C000200385

PARTY WA

and what to do with them

with them

JOHN ANSTEY
BA FRICS FCIArb

FOURTH EDITION

RICS BOOKS
for
The Royal Institution of Chartered Surveyors
12 Great George Street London SW1P 3AD

Published on behalf of
The Royal Institution of Chartered Surveyors
by RICS Books
12 Great George Street, London SW1P 3AD

Scottish Branch Office
7 Manor Place, Edinburgh EH3 7DN

First edition 1986
Second edition 1988
Third edition 1991
Fourth edition 1996

ISBN 0 85406 786 8

Illustrations by Michael Cromar

Typeset in 11pt New Baskerville by Columns Design Ltd., Reading
Printed in Great Britain by Bourne Press Ltd.

Contents

Introduction

This book deals with the *Party Wall etc. Act, 1996* as it applies to England and Wales, and it does not pretend to be an exposition of the general law.

The original edition of *Party Walls and what to do with them* was conceived when the only thing that was likely to happen to the 1939 London Building Acts (Amendment) Act, henceforth known as the LBA, was its extension to the parts other Acts cannot reach. Its gestation was interrupted, however, by the impending abolition of the GLC, so that for a long time no-one knew whether the Act was going to live on independently, or die with the Council. That Act did survive the abolition of the GLC, and now the 1996 Act has extended its benefits to the whole of England and Wales.

This is a narrative book, not an annotated Act nor a clause by clause exposition. I have sometimes paraphrased, and sometimes quoted extracts from the Act, but I have not given large chunks of it. You may sometimes need, therefore, to have a copy of the Act to hand if you are to understand my remarks. If you are to deal adequately with party wall matters as a practitioner, you will find it absolutely essential to keep the Act by you at all times. Whenever you ask a question of a real expert, his first action will always be to reach for his copy of the Act in order to check its wording precisely. You will find parts of this book very repetitious, if you read it from cover to cover. That is because I have tried to make each chapter as complete in itself as possible, without sending you backwards and forwards looking for other necessary bits of information. Nevertheless, I have cross-referenced it where I have thought that extended ancillary information elsewhere in its pages may be helpful.

Because the 1939 Act worked so well, there is not a large amount of relevant case law, but much of what there is arising from that and earlier London Building Acts will continue to be of assistance, and a great deal of what goes on is governed by convention and common sense between surveyors. A lot of this book, therefore, consists of my personal opinion as to what is right or not, and those bits are of course the most reliable. Case law tends to change, not only from case to case, but from court to court, so those bits are less reliable. I have tried to make it clear where you have my unsupported word for anything, which can therefore be taken as gospel, and where you have only legal authority for something, which should therefore only be relied upon until the next leading case.

I would welcome any arguments that readers may care to put forward against any of the views I have expressed. Some of what I have written has already been amended by my listening to the wise counsel of Eric Roe, who has kindly read the typescript, but I haven't always bowed to him, so if you still disagree with anything, blame me, not him.

In each succeeding edition of my earlier book, I dealt with most comments or suggestions sent to me by readers, as well as including some new material which has arisen from my own experience in the last couple of years. In this new work I have also incorporated that additional information where it is still relevant.

Finally, I would like to thank those whose example and assistance have inspired and enabled me to write this book: Keith McDonald, of whom every Building Surveyor has tales of help and encouragement to tell, and who has been a constant opponent and second father to me in the profession; Eric Roe, another hard opponent and great friend, on whom (as I've said before) I have already tried this stuff for size; the Building Surveyors' Secretariat at the RICS, who begged me to write something to which they could refer their constant enquiries; my father, Bryan Anstey, who first persuaded me to specialise in party walls; my brother-in-law, Michael Cromar, for providing illustrations whenever I need them; and my partners and staff for doing all my work for me so that I had the time available to write.

Chapter 1

The Appointment of Surveyors

The activities of surveyors are so central to party wall proceedings that I think it is probably helpful to deal with their appointment and their power even before dealing with the rights of owners. If there is any dispute between the owners, then it is to be 'determined in accordance with section 10' of the Act.

There are always two courses open to owners, assuming that they can't agree upon the works in the first place: to agree instead upon one surveyor to sort the matter out; or each to select a surveyor. The first option is not used as often as it might be with advantage. Since a good party wall surveyor operates in a judicious manner at all times, regardless of who appointed him – to which I shall come in greater detail shortly – it is quite easy for such a man to see that Mr Black and Mr White, even if they are wildly at odds with each other, both have their rights enforced as well as respected. Their respective rights are, indeed, very often obvious to the experienced practitioner, who has to tell one if not both of the owners that they cannot do what they would like to do.

A man so jointly selected is called an Agreed Surveyor and 'agreed' means, of course, agreed between the two owners. The words of the section are '. . . shall concur in the appointment of one surveyor'. Later on, power is given for one owner to make an appointment on behalf of another who has neglected to do so, but that does not mean (*pace* some solicitors who tried it on once in a case with which I was involved) the power to nominate your surveyor as the 'agreed' one. I have also known some owners and/or their surveyors invite an Adjoining Owner to accept them as agreed. In one particular case that springs to mind, the surveyor in question, who had quite distinctly urged concurrence upon the Adjoining Owner, turned out to be not unconnected with the Building Owner, and when the building next door began to fall down (through no fault of the surveyor, I would hasten to point out) his position, which had always been dubious in my opinion, began to look

A good party wall surveyor

distinctly uncomfortable. Since these words first appeared, the surveyor has informed me that he severed his connection with the Building Owner as soon as a conflict of interest appeared, and told the Adjoining Owner what he had done.

Quite apart from such extraordinary liaisons, I would suggest that if, when a difference is anticipated, the Building Owner nominates his intended surveyor at the same time as serving his notice, the Adjoining Owner should be quite prepared to accept that surveyor to act between the parties, provided either that the surveyor is already known to him by repute or that the works are small and the surveyor appears to be qualified to deal with them. This has happened to me more than once when, on behalf of a certain building owner, I have had to serve notice affecting properties which turned out to be owned by people or companies by whom I had previously been appointed in similar cases. They have then concurred in the selection of me as surveyor. It has also happened to me, but less often, when the party on whom notice was served, previously unknown to me, has decided that I have a nice honest face and that it would be quite safe to leave the whole matter in my hands. On only one occasion has this caused any embarrassment. In that case, the original Adjoining Owner decided in turn to redevelop and appointed me as (now) Building Owner's Surveyor. The original developer concurred in my position as Agreed Surveyor, but conflict arose when a flaw in the earlier award came to light as a result of the later work. Both parties then wanted me to side with them exclusively, which was impossible. Despite the unhappy outcome of that particular job, I will not allow this unique occurrence to deter me from accepting similar appointments.

One possible flaw in party wall procedures under the Act is that the cost of producing an award in relation to the cost of the works can be disproportionate. If the owner of a small terraced house in a small provincial town wants to carry out an improvement to his property affecting both his neighbours (even assuming that they are all freeholders, another little problem to which I shall return) the cost of paying three different surveyors could be ridiculously high, even if they were all moderate in their charges. Owners must be more ready to concur in the selection of an Agreed Surveyor, and surveyors must so comport themselves in party wall matters as to fill owners with confidence in their ability and willingness to act impartially.

Fees, too, should be tailored to the size of the job, and an appointment as Adjoining Owner's Surveyor should not be looked on as a licence to extract money from the Building Owner.

We must again return to Messrs White and Black. They are both rich men (though they will be a lot poorer by the time they've paid their surveyors for all the differences they're about to have) and they propose each to appoint their own surveyor, under Section 10(1)(b). Whom can they appoint? 'Surveyor' is not, unlike 'architect', a protected term in law, and therefore they can appoint anyone. Under the LBA, it was argued that one could appoint oneself, and on one occasion I would have been very glad if such an appointment had been made. Notice had been served on a lady; she had appointed an architect as her surveyor; I had been appointed by the Building Owner. We had – eventually – reached agreement on an award when he suddenly informed me that he, too, was an owner[1] of the property and that he had appointed another architect as his surveyor. The second one wouldn't agree

[1]   See Chapter 5 for how this comes about.

on anything that the first one, his Appointing Owner[1], had agreed to, and wouldn't even agree to the same Third Surveyor[2], so that I couldn't even guarantee a consistent result by going to that august personage. The possibility of appointing oneself, however, no longer exists, since a 'surveyor' is defined in section 20(1) as 'any person not being a party to the matter . . .', so anyone else will do: please not an accountant or a solicitor, but mother, sister, brother, aunt, or nephew would be bearable.

Let's go a little further than 'whom can you appoint?' and ask: 'whom should you appoint?' If I were to answer this question really candidly, I would give you a dozen or so names of surveyors personally known to me or, a little less restrictively, recommend you to The Pyramus and Thisbe Club[3], but perhaps I should be rather more general in a publication of this sort. A party wall surveyor should be well acquainted with the party wall procedures, because their little peculiarities, with which you are only just beginning to be acquainted, demand specialist knowledge and understanding. This, I can assure you, narrows the field very considerably. It is desirable that he should have a technical qualification, if only to impress the opposition, and he should be accustomed to dealing with structural matters, probably as architect, engineer or building surveyor.

Of course, the expertise which I am insisting on is not essential for a dispute over a boundary wall, but Messrs Black and White are beginning as I mean to go on, by assuming that appalling complications are going to arise, and that therefore only the best original choices will do. They may know someone suitable, or know someone who knows someone, or they can ask one of the professional institutions for some suggestions. Never forget, however, that I strongly recommend concurring on an Agreed Surveyor if possible.

One further matter. In the early years of the Act's operation, there are likely to be more surveyors based in London who are familiar with party wall matters, but there can be no justification for appointing someone from the metropolis, whose every visit to the site is going to involve three hours travelling time, unless it is quite clear that provincial gentlemen are not suitably qualified. If someone other than a local man is appointed, he should not expect to charge for travelling to the distant site (and nor should a provincial

[1]   And see Chapter 4 for the reason for this expression.
[2]   Not long to wait to hear about him: see next page or two.
[3]   For a description of this eminent body, see Appendix V.

gentleman charge for travelling to London) while his rates should be commensurate with the job, rather than his metropolitan expectations.

By the way, the Act says 'appoint a surveyor'. It does not say 'appoint a firm of surveyors'. You cannot therefore appoint 'Messrs Bright Sheep and Woolly', or even 'a partner in Quite Blank and Abruptly', although I suppose it might just be all right to nominate 'the senior partner in Wilson Keppell and Betty', since that would be a particular individual. It is much better, however to appoint Mr Betty by name, if that is who you want.

Let us suppose that Mr Black appoints Mr L. Armstrong as his surveyor, and Mr White appoints Mr E. Caruso, thus ensuring plenty of attention for two of my heroes. What is the first thing that these two must do? It is not, as so many seem to think, to meet and agree a schedule of condition[1], or start discussing an award[2], or even, which is regrettably uppermost in some so-called professionals' minds, negotiate their fees. It is, in fact, to select a Third Surveyor. So much is this a part of the initial process, that it is made part of the same sub-section, 10(1)(b): 'each party shall appoint a surveyor and the two surveyors so appointed shall forthwith select a third surveyor'. There is very good reason for this. At the outset, there should be no friction between the surveyors on any point – in theory there should never be any friction between them but in practice there often is – and it should be comparatively easy to choose the umpire. If they wait until there is a point needing the umpire's decision, they may not be able to agree on anything, including the umpire's name.

The same strictures, only more so, apply to the selection of Third Surveyors as to the first two. There are many people whom I am quite happy to meet as 'the other surveyor', but whom I would not be enthusiastic about being called to sit in judgement on a knotty point. I suppose that there are, as I write, no more than about half a dozen people whose names are regularly put forward and accepted by serious practitioners in party wall matters. I regret to say that, all too often, people who should know better put forward as potential Third Surveyors men or women whom I would not trust to tell me the time of day. You should only need a Third Surveyor in exceptionally tricky circumstances, and your selected

[1] See Chapter 4.
[2] See Chapter 6.

13

arbiter therefore must be capable of dealing with difficult and uncommon situations. It's not a sinecure. It is usual for the Building Owner's Surveyor to suggest three names, and for the Adjoining Owner's Surveyor to select one of them[1]. In our case, Mr Armstrong might suggest Mr J. Louis, Mr H. Cooper or Mr C. Clay, and Mr Caruso choose the last named.

What happens if the first two surveyors, even at the outset, cannot agree upon a Third Surveyor, so that even when offered such a rich choice as that put forward by Mr Armstrong, Mr Caruso is happy with none of them, and suggests instead Mr J. McCormack, Mr W. Midgley, or Mr B. Gigli? Mr Armstrong likes none of them, and no other names that he suggests (Mr J. Teagarden, Mr B. Freeman or Mr F. Waller) are any more acceptable. The writers of the Act have at least thought of this eventuality: either or both parties can apply to the 'Appointing Officer', a person so chosen by the local authority, to nominate the Third Surveyor, who might even choose a lady to fill the role: perhaps the divine Emma Kirkby.

While the GLC existed, there was an officer known as the 'Superintending Architect', one of whose minor functions was to appoint Third Surveyors. Another distinguished building surveyor (Donald Ensom) and I approached the GLC, offering to cast our eyes over the Superintending Architect's list of potential Third Surveyors and offer suggestions for addition, revision and excision. We were eventually sent a copy of a two column list: at the head of the left-hand column 'Donald Ensom'; at the head of the right 'John Anstey'. We felt that no further comment was required.

An appointment by the Appointing Officer is final – he could even appoint someone already rejected by one of the parties – and the surveyor so appointed is in exactly the same position as one agreed upon by the other two. Exactly the same procedure is followed if either party refuses to agree, or fails for ten days to answer a formal request to agree upon a Third Surveyor. The phrase used, 'refuses or for ten days after a written request neglects to . . .', appears quite often in section 10 and is examined in more detail elsewhere[2].

Don't, I would suggest, write to your chosen Third Surveyor and tell him you've selected him. Don't even ask him if you may

---

[1] See *Party Wall Legislation and Procedure*, published by RICS Books, for a form for this purpose.
[2] Later in this chapter.

select him. You're probably not going to need him, so you're wasting his time by writing to him now. He can't tell at this juncture whether he will be available to act when and if you have a dispute. He might be free now, but just starting a High Court case or a holiday at the time your disagreement reaches a head. So wait till he's actually needed before popping the question. It may well be a politeness to ask a chap if he minds, in general, your putting his name forward as Third Surveyor, but speaking for myself, I would prefer you to do it by telephone.

Special offer: anyone who has bought this book has my permission to put my name forward; anyone who has borrowed this book or is reading it in the library has to ask by phone.

If the Third Surveyor dies, becomes incapable, refuses, or neglects to act, then we go back to square one and start trying to select another man acceptable to both the first two. Perhaps Mr Armstrong and Mr Caruso will jointly agree on Mr Cooper this time, but if not then re-read the relevant pages for procedure as before.

One thing must be made very clear. Once a surveyor has been appointed under the Act, whether as Agreed Surveyor or as any other kind, then he must forthwith adopt a judicial and impartial attitude to the settlement of disputes. In some cases he may have previously been acting as the agent of his client, at the very least perhaps in the service of notices, and in some matters he may well continue to do so, but in all matters where he is acting in his capacity as a party wall surveyor he must be an arbitrator, not an agent. It is implicit in the whole way that Section 10 is drawn that the surveyors are to work together to settle matters, not in opposition to each other[1]. It is particularly difficult for an architect, who may well be expected by his client to deal with party wall matters on a small job as part of his general duties, to switch from the impassioned agent seeking the speedy and inexpensive completion of his beautiful design to the disinterested surveyor equally ready to heed the needs of the next-door neighbour, and thus perhaps protract the job while adding to its cost. Difficult it may be, but he must do it, if he is properly to fulfil his function under the Act.

There are various provisions for ensuring that the surveyors get on with their work, or for replacing them if they cease to act, to which I shall come in due course, but there is one eventuality which

---

[1] And see *Selby* v *Whitbread*, Chapter 16.

15

is conspicuous by its absence. There is no power given to a dissatisfied owner to discharge his surveyor. Under the LBA this was implicit, but section 10(2) of the new Act makes it explicit. This is important for two reasons: firstly, it emphasises yet again the necessity for impartiality in the surveyor; and secondly, it makes it impossible for a deliberately obstructive owner to frustrate the purposes of the Act by constantly hiring and firing surveyors, thus regularly causing proceedings to start *de novo*.

The only ways in which a surveyor can cease to be the appointed surveyor are: if the job comes to an end (not stated in the Act but, *pace Marchant* v *Capital and Counties*[1], surely obviously so when any making good has been completed); if he dies (and even one of my Appointing Owners, who rang the RICS to know how he could get rid of a surveyor who refused to do what he was told, didn't go so far as to promote that end); or if he becomes incapable of acting. Both the latter eventualities are provided for by section 10(5).

'Incapable of acting' will bear a little examination. One of my staff once gave notice, under the Party Wall Surveyors Act, 1975[2], that he intended to leave my office by more than six metres, and therefore called upon me to appoint another surveyor in his stead. I replied that, as he had always been incapable of acting, I couldn't see how his departure would change things. I knew what I meant: but what does the Act mean? Clearly a building surveyor who proposed to become a quantity surveyor would qualify, since his removal by men in white coats could only be a matter of time, but would a chap who went off for four weeks' holiday be incapable, or merely neglectful? It is, in fact a critical difference, since if he is incapable, the owner who appointed him can appoint another in his place, but if he is neglectful, then the other surveyor can proceed *ex parte*. This will have to be considered below, but meanwhile we must concentrate on 'incapable'.

This is another instance where something which was implicit in the LBA has become explicit in the present Act. Whereas it used to be believed to be in order for a surveyor to inform his Appointing Owner that he was incapable of acting, no one was sure if his statement to that effect was legally adequate. Section 10(5) now specifically allows for the surveyor to deem himself incapable. Very rarely is his incapability a physical or a mental inability to cope, I am

---

[1]   See Chapter 16.
[2]   A joke.

happy to say. Far more often it is a diplomatic sickness of some kind. As I have already explained, an appointment is specific to one person: you cannot appoint a firm. Sometimes the named surveyor changes firms in the middle of a job, and what happens then depends upon the terms on which this transfer takes place. Strictly speaking, I think that a firm could not stop him retaining the party wall appointment, and sometimes they have no wish to do so, so that the appointment moves with him to his new place of employment. At other times, either because the firm he leaves is in a position to exert strong pressure on him in other respects, or because it would not in fact be convenient for him to retain the appointment, the surveyor notifies his Appointing Owner that he is no longer capable of acting in the matter.

In such cases, the outgoing surveyor usually suggests that the bereaved owner may care to appoint Mr T. Schipa, the man most suitable in the original firm to take over the work, but in fact there is no obligation upon the owner to do so.

Sometimes the owner will not wish to appoint anyone else from the same firm. This is particularly likely to be true if the incapability is the result of another kind of diplomatic action. As stated above, the disgruntled owner cannot sack his surveyor and, if his nerves are as strong as his sense of justice, the surveyor can go on acting even for an owner who detests and distrusts him, but very often he may feel that the best way out for both parties is for him to become incapable of acting, and thus allow the owner another choice. It is my experience, however, that this kind of conflict usually arises when the owner wilfully refuses to understand the Act and the surveyor's position under it, and in that case his second choice, if the latter is himself a proper party wall surveyor, is likely to prove just as unsatisfactory as the first, since he, too, will refuse to 'do what the client tells him', such as acting improperly in trying to obstruct the other owner's rights.

However the vacancy arises, whether by death or incapability – diplomatic or otherwise – under section 10(5) the 'surveyorless' owner can appoint anyone he likes to fill the gap, and the new man will 'have the same power and authority' as his predecessor. I suppose that, despite the Act's silence on the point, the owner could even at this stage change his mind and concur in the selection of the remaining surveyor, but I have never known it done.

The other matter on which the Act is silent and which is relevant at this point is: how bound is the successor by his predecessor's actions? This question arises in a similar form, and will have to be considered later[1], when dealing with changes in ownership of properties which are already involved in party wall proceedings. Once again, I can only quote my own views, and I think that any late arrival must be bound by concluded events, but free to go his own way on matters which are not yet settled. I can see that he might wish to agree upon a different Third Surveyor, but I also think that unless the other surveyor agreed to a change, an existing decision would stand. This is the matter I am least sure about, however, and I am far more secure in my opinion that the newcomer would be bound by an agreed schedule of condition, and certain that he would have to accept a signed award; I think that he would have the right to change an award which was still in draft. Note that if an 'Agreed Surveyor' fails to get on with things, or becomes incapable (or dies), the whole proceedings start *de novo*, so that the Adjoining Owner is not bound to concur in the Building Owner's new suggestion. If he was happy with the first man, but is not happy with the second, he can put forward his own surveyor under 10(1)(b) just as he had the power to do in the original situation.

Suppose that the Adjoining Owner won't do anything: what then? It almost always is the Adjoining Owner who neglects to act, of course, although very occasionally you may find a Building Owner pressing on with work and refusing to appoint a surveyor. In most cases, a Building Owner who won't appoint a surveyor won't have served a notice either, but I did receive a belated and ill-scrawled notice recently on which the illegible Building Owner had written 'n/a' (presumably meaning 'not applicable') where he should have inserted the name of his surveyor. Most Adjoining Owners would seek an injunction as a remedy in that case, but if a notice had been served they could opt to appoint a surveyor on behalf of the Building Owner, who could then make an award binding the Building Owner to be a good boy for the rest of the works. This, however, is unlikely, and the speculation is forcing us to get ahead of ourselves. *Revenons à nos moutons.*

If either party refuses to appoint a surveyor or, you won't be surprised to hear, neglects to do so for ten days after a written request, the other party has the power to make the appointment for him. The usual pattern is that the Building Owner serves a notice[2];

---

[1]   See Chapter 11.
[2]   See Chapter 5.

the Adjoining Owner is silent; fourteen days later the Building Owner requests the Adjoining Owner to appoint a surveyor, since a dispute is deemed to have arisen; Brer Rabbit, he still lies low and says nothing; so the Building Owner now chooses a surveyor for him.

When choosing a surveyor for someone else you should use the same care as if you were choosing him for yourself. I have never known an award set aside because one owner chose a bad egg as the other owner's surveyor, but I should think it was distinctly possible. So choose well. Of course, it's perfectly proper to choose someone who is already involved in the job, either acting for another interest in the same building, or for another building adjoining the development. It must be cheaper, and there's nothing improper in that, by saving travelling time, and time arguing the same problems with several different surveyors. If no suitable candidate is already in the vicinity, then use the criteria set out above and choose a suitable man for the particular job.

Remember that your selection on behalf of the Adjoining Owner is no more your creature than he would be if he were your own appointment as your surveyor. I was once appointed thus, and the Building Owner said, 'Right: we can get on with it now, can't we?' I disillusioned him, and proceeded to deal critically with his proposals, insisting on several changes for the benefit of 'my' owner. Sadly, but not surprisingly in this wicked world, I got no more work from that source for several years.

I think I have now covered every eventuality except one, arising out of the appointment of surveyors, and I never before realised how much could be said on the subject. The one remaining possibility I have already alluded to briefly, and it arises when an appointed surveyor fails or refuses to act. In that case (section 10(6)), the other surveyor may proceed *ex parte*: that is to say that he may draft his own award and issue it, with all the force as if it had been agreed by the two surveyors, but again the proper disinterest must be shown. The award must not confer all rights on one owner while neglecting those of the other. It must be one which you would probably have agreed with the other chap, if only he could have been bothered to do so.

It has been known for surveyors to listen too much to their Appointing Owners, and deliberately to put off signing an award because 'they were told to'. In such cases, it can have a salutary effect on them – and their owners – to issue an *ex parte* award. Apart from anything else, they can see their fees disappearing, and that often talks to such time-servers. They almost always then rush back into action, usually challenging the validity of the *ex parte* award. When that happens to me, I always refuse to withdraw the award, which I wouldn't have made if it hadn't been justified and in order, but I will often agree to succeed it, not supplant it, by a bi-partisan award. What's more, the second award rarely differs from the first by more than a few words of little consequence.

Perhaps I ought to close this chapter by telling you what an 'Owner' is. He is defined as including:

a) 'a person in receipt of . . . the rents or profits of land[1];
b) 'a person in possession of land otherwise than as a mortgagee or as a tenant from year to year . . .';
c) 'a purchaser of an interest in land under a contract for purchase or under an agreement for a lease . . .'

A Building Owner is the one who intends to do any work, exercising his rights or incurring obligations under the Act, and an Adjoining Owner owns or occupies 'land, buildings, storeys or rooms adjoining those of the Building Owner'. The word 'adjoining' is defined to include any property within 3 metres or 6 metres when the provisions of section 6 come into play[1]. Each and every 'owner' is entitled to his surveyor.

Now we have one or two (and if two, three) surveyors, and we know how to appoint them (in writing, by the way, see section 10(2)), replace them, and that we can't displace them. What have we got them for? Read on.

---

[1]   See Chapter 3.

Chapter 2

What is a Party Wall?

I can never ask a question like that, even of myself, without hearing that awful music that used to accompany a dreadful recitation of the merits of a 'boy' or a 'girl' or some such ghastly abstraction in pop records of the fifties or thereabouts. Fortunately for you, dear reader, the answer to the question above will only come accompanied by whatever rubbish you're listening to on the radio while you should be concentrating whole-heartedly on this learned work. As a matter of fact, it is very easy to tell you what a party wall is, as long as we make it clear that we're only dealing with the Act. It is either a wall standing on the land of two owners, or else however much of a wall separates the buildings of two owners. That's fairly simple, but I'll trot out my standard illustrations again just to make it even clearer.

The first thing to note is that the wall doesn't have to be equally astride the boundary. I suppose that the courts might decide that

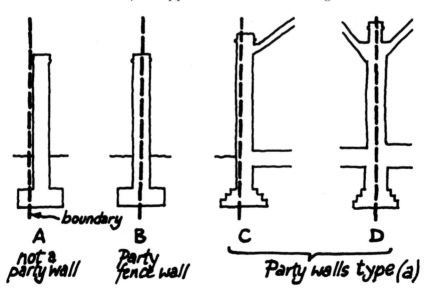

A
not a
party wall

B
Party
fence wall

C

D

boundary

Party walls type (a)

21

half an inch in a three foot thick wall was a tiny mistake in what was obviously intended to be a wall wholly on the land of one owner, but next week, as I write these words, or yesterday, as I pick up my pen again after breaking off at that point, there is/was a case being heard in the High Court which included the question as to whether a wall sitting one and a half inches on one side of a boundary and seven and a half inches on the other was meant to be astride it or a *de minimis* error in setting out[1].

The second thing to note is that I have given an over-simplification of the definition of a party wall in section 20, which makes it clear that the 'astrideness' does not include 'the projection of any artificially formed support on which the wall rests . . .'. I have always taken that to refer to foundations, howsoever formed, whether of stepped brick footings or concrete – not, however, reinforced concrete[2] – but I have also heard the argument advanced that this includes piers. Apart from the fact that I don't think walls can be said to rest on piers, it is noteworthy that section 2(2)(g), of which more – not much more – later, does not specifically mention piers as something which may be cut off in order to allow the raising of another wall, and sub-section (h) also refers to 'parts of any wall or building . . . overhanging' the next-door land, which also doesn't sound much like what a pier does. Nevertheless, my inclination is to believe that piers[3], provided that is all they are, and that they do not form a substantial part of the wall, should be excluded from the determination of the boundary and included within those things which may be cut off.

Nomenclature is a tricky business when dealing with party walls.

The subtle difference, which you will immediately spot, between these diagrams and those at the beginning of the chapter, is that if a party wall is type (a), standing astride the boundary, then all the wall above it is a party wall, whereas if it stands wholly on the land of one owner, type (b), it ceases to be a party wall as soon as next-door no longer encloses on it. Sideways extensions have the same status, or lack of it. Remember that in this sub-section, (b), we're only dealing with walls which stand wholly on the land of one

---

[1]   The judge held that the measurements were too approximate for him to put the wall anywhere exact.
[2]   See Chapter 3.
[3]   See Chapter 3.

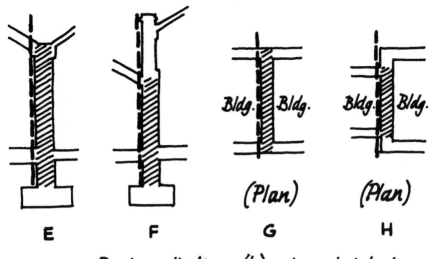

E   F   G   H

Party walls type (b) shown hatched

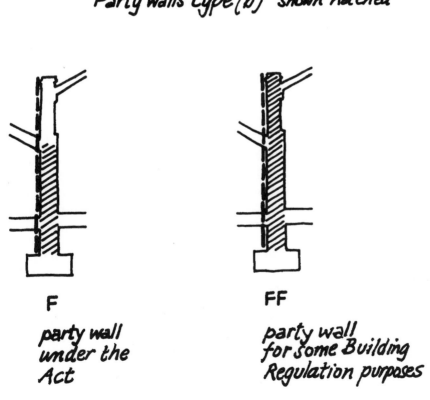

F

party wall
under the
Act

FF

party wall
for some Building
Regulation purposes

owner, but which happen also to form, wholly or partly, an enclosure for a neighbouring building. A wall standing wholly on one owner's land, acting as a garden wall only, which has been used as an enclosing wall for a building by an Adjoining Owner does not fall within either definition: it is therefore not a party wall, but I don't know what it is instead.

The question has been asked: for how long does a wall have to be enclosed on before it becomes a party wall type (b)? Can a chap sneak up behind your wall when you're not looking, slap his lean-to up against your wall, and proudly proclaim that you now can't do anything to it without his say-so? I know – yet again – of no legal authority on the point, but learned counsel in a talk to The Pyramus and Thisbe Club[1] expressed the opinion that you would have the normal limitation period of six years in which to call upon the propped-up character to abate his trespass. Less reliable persons have put forward the suggestion that as soon as he makes his enclosure he is safe, but this seems ridiculous to me. There may be more merit in the argument that you need to acquire an adverse possessory (or squatter's) title over twelve years. It may even be argued that you can never attain party wallhood, since to butt your

[1] See Appendix V.

building against someone else's wall is a trespass: a continuing trespass as long as it's there, so that there is a continuing right of action as long as it remains there. I suppose that, since a right of support can be acquired by prescription, after twenty years you can at least rely on not being allowed to fall down.

Probably a safe rule for those acquiring rights is not to think you're safe until twelve or twenty years have elapsed, and for those enclosed against to fear the worst after six.

There are other definitions, too, some of which, to my mind, lack absolute certainty, but one at least is crystal clear. A 'party fence wall' complies with definition (a) but has no buildings attached to it, on either side. It is therefore most commonly found in what we might call 'garden walls', standing half on each of two gardens, front or back.

Also of general application is the term 'party structure'. This is so general that it includes party walls (and, I would think, though it is not specifically stated, party fence walls) and also 'a floor partition or other structure separating buildings or parts of buildings approached solely by separate staircases or separate entrances'. The words 'from without' used to appear at the end of this definition in the LBA, which led to ambiguity, or at any rate to anomaly. What was the structure between the different floors of a block of flats? The flats are served by a common stair, although their front doors, on to corridors, might be argued to be 'from without'. But take a converted mansion in which the semi-basement (or garden flat, as it will probably be called in the sale particulars) has been severed from the ground floor, had its staircase removed, and been provided with its own front door to the outside world. Now the ceiling/floor (depending upon which way you're looking) is party, though it is unlikely to differ in construction or impact upon the parties from the structure separating the ground and first floors which, following the argument adduced above, will not be party.

For that reason, it was thought desirable in the new Act to include all such horizontal separating structures. Note that it does not attempt to define ownership of such divisions, and solicitors can continue happily to debate whether title extends to the joists or the floor coverings.

The term 'boundary wall' appears from time to time in the Act, but is not defined except by exclusion. At Section 1(1) remarks are made about 'a boundary wall (not being a party fence wall or the external wall of a building)' and by extrapolation it would appear that a boundary wall is a fence wall standing wholly on the land of one owner. Similarly, 'the external wall of a building' appears to be one standing wholly on the land of the owner of the building attached to it. If there is open space the other side of the wall, then there are no party wall incidents, but of course if there is some other building attached to all or part of it, then it comes into type (b). One kind of wall has no term of art applied to it at all (even if you can dignify 'external wall of a building' with that title), and needs one. That is the kind which figured in *Gyle-Thompson* v *Walstreet*[1], and is illustrated a little further on as a 'whatcha call it?'

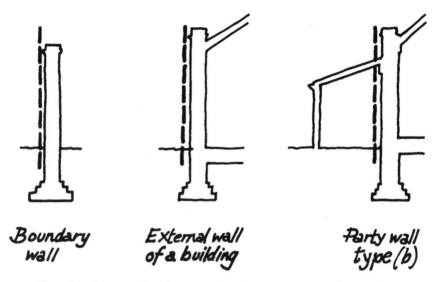

Boundary wall

External wall of a building

Party wall type (b)

You should note, by the way, that because a type (b) wall is only 'party' where the two buildings are separated, many of the rights granted under section 2 do not apply. The person on whose land the wall does not stand cannot, for example, raise it. Furthermore, it probably stops being party if the non-owner demolishes his building which has been constructed against it without immediately rebuilding.

What do you call a wall which stands on the land of two owners, but serves only one building, as in Fig (c) on p21? 'A party wall' is a perfectly correct answer, since it stands on the land of two owners, but it doesn't clearly enough discriminate from the more usual

[1]   See Chapter 16.

kind, as in Fig (d) on p21 and from 'the external wall of a building', which it most certainly is in common parlance.

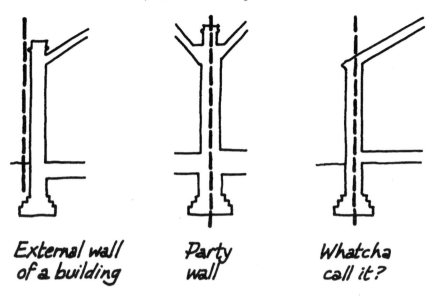

External wall of a building   **Party wall**   **Whatcha call it?**

In my earlier book, I speculated about the possibility of the London Building Acts (Amendment) Act 1996, or even – *mirabile dictu*, the national Party Wall Act, 2000 – and hoped that separate definitions and clarification would be added to these latter kinds of structure. Sadly, despite my intimate involvement with the drafting of the present Act, we failed to invent terms of art for these curiosities.

Chapter 3

Rights of Owners – and Duties!

Section 2

The first thing to note is that one tends to speak of section 2 as conferring rights – but some of those rights would be there without the Act, and those items thus become restrictions on the owner, since he cannot do those things without notice, any more than he can do the things for which he specifically needs the power of the Act.

The second thing to note is the subtle difference between 2(2)(b) and 2(2)(e). Much of the wording is similar, but clause (b) is concerned with works which are 'necessary on account of defect or want of repair'. This may make a crucial difference to who pays for it, so be careful when serving notice which one you cite, and take care when you receive a notice to observe which one has been used.

Clause (a) permits underpinning, thickening or raising a party structure, clause (b) allows demolition of a defective one, and clause (e) deals with rebuilding stronger or higher simply because the Building Owner needs it. In the case of actions under most of the clauses of section 2(2) there is a specific requirement that any damage to next door should be made good. Raising has been held to include going downwards, to form a basement. In addition, any chimney stacks or flues against the wall must be raised sufficiently to keep them drawing.

As remarked above, the works in these clauses include 'thickening', which is something you would normally expect to be able to do without reference to the chap next door (and which, when it is done, is probably so done) but technically you are required to serve notice that you intend to do so. Even 'making good' and 'repairing' need notice, though perhaps more in order to safeguard the apportionment of payment than for any other reason. I was recently asked if you needed to serve notice under the

Act if you were intending merely to repoint your side of a party wall. I should think that the strict legal answer is yes, but you could probably obtain your neighbour's consent to the work by friendly discussion.

The extent of the right given by clause (e) is really quite staggering. The Adjoining Owner can be sitting on his side of the party wall, quietly drinking his tea, dictating to his secretary, beating his wife, or whatever takes his fancy, when suddenly there flops on to his doormat a letter telling him that in two months all these clandestine activities (the tea drinking, for example) are going to be revealed to the world because the man next door, who has suddenly been elevated to the status of a Building Owner, has decided that the wall between them is of insufficient strength or height for the purposes of his 'intended building'. Our innocent can, of course, usually have some screens installed at the Building Owner's expense before the demolition commences, and 'all damage occasioned by the work to the adjoining premises or to their internal finishings and decorations' will have to be made good out of the same pocket: but the disruption, the upheaval, not once but twice (when the screens go in and when they come out again) is likely to try him sorely – and although there is provision in the Act for soothing that hurt, at section 11(6)[1], it is unlikely fully to make up for everything.

There is one dramatic change in this section, compared with the LBA. Certain surveyors were of the opinion that if one side had paid for the erection of a high wall, astride their boundary, which the other side only used as a garden wall, the Building Owner was entitled to take down the wall and rebuild it to a lesser height, provided that it still served the needs of the Adjoining Owner. This led to the case of *Gyle-Thompson* v *Walstreet*[2] where the judge held that he couldn't. As this seemed patently unfair, the present Act has specifically incorporated such a right under (m). Clause (f) is another one which gives an owner a right which he may have been under the impression he already had: 'to cut into a party structure'. It doesn't say what this cutting in may be for. Usually when notice is served it is a matter of bonding in a new partition wall, or providing the bearing for a beam, but the installation of a wall safe and, specifically, the provision of a damp proof course are also covered. Decorations have to be made good (again) as they do in clause (g),

[1] See Chapter 10.
[2] See Chapter 16.

which really does give the Building Owner a right which he otherwise wouldn't have, and (h) takes it even further. He can cut off almost anything which projects on or over his land, whether it's a footing, a flue, or a leaning wall, if it gets in the way of his erecting a vertical wall against the existing structure, although one learned authority doubts whether one can be altogether ruthless with a leaning wall. He can also (under the new Act) similarly cut off anything overhanging the party wall which inhibits its raising.

Would that there were more clauses like (k), which confers a right to do 'any other necessary works' – but unfortunately limits itself to 'the connection of a party structure with the premises adjoining it'. It's not quite clear what this is meant to cover, but it is usually taken to mean things like bonding in new cross walls or front and rear walls to the party wall. However, it has recently come to be very useful for the times when an old party wall has to be left up to protect a building which is not itself properly tied into it, because the party wall originally formed part of the building which is now being demolished, while the later building (now to remain) was merely butted up against it, and perhaps block-bonded at front and rear. Despite clause (e)[1], it is often preferable not to take full advantage of this right, and to leave the old party wall in place, while building an independent wall for the new building. But then the problem arises: how is one to hold the old wall in place until the new wall gets up? Answer: clause (k), and fix the wall back to the continuing structure with tie rods, bolts, brackets, or whatever is necessary.

Clause (l) allows you to change the party fence wall into a party wall, with or without rebuilding, or to raise a party fence wall, or, very exceptionally, to knock it down, even if it is in perfect repair, and rebuild it again just, it would appear, to satisfy a whim.

Clause (m) spells out in detail the right to reduce a party wall in height. The Building Owner can do so to a minimum height of two metres (ample for a garden wall for next door) or to the height currently enclosed on by the Adjoining Owner. This will be taken to include any necessary parapet, by sub-section (7).

Finally, clause (n) allows the exposure of a party wall to the elements (by demolishing one's building which used it for enclosure) only if adequate weathering is provided. Adequacy will depend on the wall, the exposure, and the time for which it is likely to endure.

[1] See above.

30

Actually, it isn't finally, because I have omitted clauses (c) and (d) and haven't yet reached sub-section (3), but this detailed exposition can be so wearying that I thought I'd better put in a false summit where you could rest for a bit. The reason that I've not yet dealt with (c) and (d) is that in all my experience, I've never had to use either of them. Furthermore, I'm not sure how consistent they are with sub-section (8). Clauses (c) and (d) are all about altering structures which don't comply with the statutory requirements, while sub-section (8) says that anything built before the Acts shall be deemed to comply, providing it complied with whatever was in force when it was built. If so, why should anyone want to waste money on making something comply with the newer enactments? All I can say, I suppose, is that if someone feels the urge to demolish timber 'party walls', or raise fallen arches, then they can do so by following the usual procedures. However, I suppose that the local authority under the new legislation might instruct the Building Owner to do the work, and the latter would then have to serve notice under one or more of these sub-sections.

Sub-sections (3) to (6) deal with the responsibility for making good, arising out of the exercise of the various options above.

It is perhaps worth mentioning here, though you won't reach it in the Act until section 7(4), that you cannot place reinforced concrete on next-door's land without written consent, and that consent must come from the Adjoining Owner, not his surveyor.

Section 6

Section 6 is curious in its differences from section 2: you can pull down a wall which reveals next door in all its nakedness without producing any plans of your proposals – or at any rate you can serve notice of your intention to do so: the surveyors will soon enough insist on the plans – but you cannot serve notice of your intention to build an independent building whose foundations may impinge upon an Adjoining Owner without accompanying it with a plan of your site and a section showing the depth to which you intend to excavate. Strange, isn't it? Many people seem to think you have a duty to show the depth of next-door's foundations, but the Act doesn't say so.

I must now trot out my standard pictures to illustrate what used to be the Ten Foot and Twenty Foot provisions, and are now Three Metre and Six Metre provisions, on the next page.

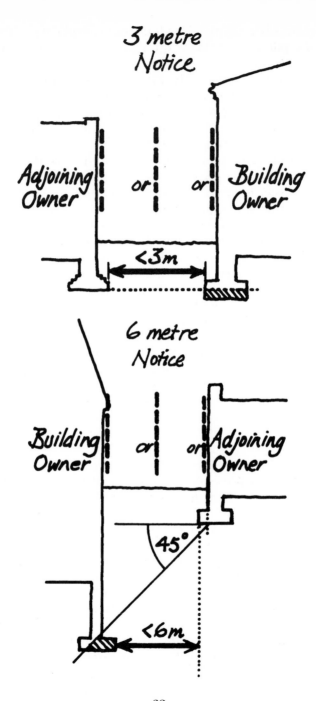

In the old LBA, the word 'independent' appeared in different places in the paragraphs that are now sub-sections (1) and (2) of section 6. This made the provisions hard to understand, and sometimes pointlessly negated the whole purpose of the section. The word has therefore been removed from the new Act. Furthermore, it seemed to those drafting the new provisions that it was illogical for a nearby property not to be served with notice simply because a narrow strip of someone else's land intervened. This was often the case in the City of London, where Twenty Foot (old style) Notices were not legally necessary across alleys belonging to the City Corporation rather than the frontagers. Section 6(4) therefore now states that anyone within the distances specified qualifies for notice, regardless of how many ownerships there may be between. A series of five metre shop frontages would consequently involve notice, if the six metre provisions applied, to both next door and next door but one.

Only occasionally does the precise measurement of the six metres cause a problem, but you must be sure where the 45° angle is drawn from, and it is as shown: where the downward projected face of the Adjoining Owner's wall meets the bottom of his foundations. If any part of the proposed building, which can include foundations, retaining walls, and may even include drains, cuts that 45° line, then notice is necessary. While we're on precision, note also where the three metres is measured: not from wall to wall, but from nearest bit of foundation to ditto. In both cases the distance is to be measured horizontally, which was believed to be the case under the LBA, though not explicitly stated. In this Act it is.

By the way, the three metres or six metres can be measured in any horizontal direction, not necessarily at right angles to the boundary. This section is of course entirely restricting a Building Owner, not conferring a right. Formerly, he could do either of these kinds of work without so much as a by your leave. Now, he not only has to give notice, he also has to say in advance what he intends to do about 'safeguarding' the Adjoining Owner's foundations. In my opinion, by far the best safeguarding of an Adjoining Owner's foundations is to leave them alone. It is preferable to design foundations so that no load is imposed on the neighbours' building or on the ground nearby in such a way that no effect is likely. I also prefer to retain the soil in the vicinity of the adjoining property by shoring or strutting, rather than expose the foundations and underpin them. If a building is underpinned there is almost inevitably some movement, albeit small, but if it can be adequately retained there may be none. There will doubtless be discussion between the surveyors on the best method in any particular case, to be settled in the usual way.

Section 1

Although this section, as the more numerate among you will have observed, comes before sections 2 and 6, it is far less frequently met with, and I have therefore relegated it to the Third Division. Here we meet the 'boundary wall', which is not defined, but which may be deduced to be a wall standing wholly on the land of one owner and not forming part of a building – a sort of unparty fence wall. If that is all that is standing on the line of junction of the lands of two owners, a Building Owner can suggest, by notice, building a party wall or party fence wall astride the boundary. If the Adjoining Owner doesn't like the idea, then the Building Owner has to place it on his own land, but he has an absolute right to put foundations (as long as they're not reinforced) on next-door's land, with due notice. This does not, however, authorise a Building Owner to knock down an Adjoining Owner's boundary wall to replace it with a party fence wall or a party wall, and so the prior existence of a boundary wall or the external wall of a building on the Adjoining Owner's land would seem to pre-empt the possible construction of a party wall.

The nationwide extension of the Act puts an end to the possibility of the recurrence of an entertaining saga related by a member of The Pyramus and Thisbe Club, Dov Kritzler – except, I suppose, on the Scottish border. A certain Building Owner served notice of his intention to build a wall on his own land with foundations protruding on to next-door's garden. He received an indignant reply telling him that he couldn't. He responded by pointing out his rights under the Act. The reply asked what that had to do with it. 'We live in the area of the Act,' said the Building Owner, 'and so you're bound to let me do it.' 'You may,' retorted the adjoining owner[1], 'but I don't.' Result, foundations on the Building Owner's land only. Obviously, the right cannot run beyond the actual boundary of the Act's operations, which in this case was the junction of the two gardens.

Take careful note that section 1 carries with it many other sections of the Act, including rights of access under section 8 and the possibility of awards under section 10.

---

[1] Note that he doesn't get capital letters, because he's outside the Act.

Chapter 4

How to have a Party Wall Affair

My learned friend, Eric Roe, said to me, *à propos* of this book: 'Whatever you do, explain the practical way things are done'. This chapter, with much attendant risk of repeating whole chunks of other chapters, will be an attempt to describe, practically, the progress of a typical party wall job.

All too typically will come a telephone call from a client – and a client he is at this stage – telling you that he's starting work tomorrow and asking you to deal with the party walls. The first thing you must do is to stop him, and then you can start sorting him out. Find out, if necessary by having a meeting with him and his architect – perhaps his engineer too – exactly what he proposes to do; extract, invariably with difficulty, details of the proposed foundations; decide which sections of the Act are relevant; tell the client (he still is) how long he must wait while notices are served; get a letter of authority from him allowing you to serve notices on his behalf, which you may well be asked by the Adjoining Owner's Surveyor to produce as evidence of that authority (see draft letter 1 in *Party Wall Legislation and Procedure* (RICS Books)); get the necessary drawings from the architect and engineer; find out who all the Adjoining Owners are; serve notice on them all, accompanied by a letter on the lines of RICS draft letter 3; and then sit back and wait. You're actually waiting for two things: the anguished cries of 'Can't I start yet?' from your (still) client; and the responses from the Adjoining Owners. As soon as you get those (ignore the anguished cries) and assuming that they don't consent to the works, a dispute has arisen and you become – proud moment – a party wall surveyor. At this point, so far as matters connected with the party wall are concerned you no longer have a client: your erstwhile client is now your Appointing Owner.

Let us assume that we are carrying out works under section 2. After a fortnight, probably half the Adjoining Owners will have replied, but the others have now dissented by their silence. Three-quarters of the half who have replied will have named their surveyor. What is the minimum number of Adjoining Owners in this example?[1] To the remaining quarter you write politely pointing out that they must appoint someone, but to the other half you write more in the form of RICS draft letter 4, which reminds them that they've had a notice, and tells them what they should be doing about it.

After a bit more of this sort of stuff, you should end up with a clutch of Adjoining Owners' Surveyors. (Clutch is the right collective noun, I think, for a bunch of surveyors sitting like Humpty Dumpty on a wall). The first thing you must do is to agree upon a Third Surveyor. It's probably a good idea to try to have the same Third Surveyor for the whole site, but quite likely that each Adjoining Owner's Surveyor will have his own pet likes and dislikes among the ranks of suitable candidates. Anyway, get him or them selected, and then you can get down to the affair proper.

As your Appointing Owner (remember he is no longer your client) has been champing at the bit for several weeks already, he is almost certainly going to get on with any works of demolition straight away. Demolition needs no notice, but it can cause a lot of damage, and so it is essential to get the schedules of condition under way. As the named surveyor, you are probably above such petty matters, but you will have your leg-men to do them for you.

Some surveyors think that it is the duty of the named surveyor to do every last little part of the proceedings himself. Though they have a point, I think they are wrong. I would sympathise greatly with them if the assistants they had to deal with had no authority from 'the surveyor' to make any decisions, and had to report every least detail for higher judgement, but if 'the surveyor' only sends out assistants who are not only permitted to use, but also capable of using, their own judgement, and provided that the big man will always involve himself in any situation whose gravity demands it, then I think that devolution is perfectly proper. The Pyramus and Thisbe Club debated delegation at one meeting, and decided that while Third Surveyor duties should never be passed down the line to the third assistant, it was quite in order for almost all other work to be carried out by juniors. It was agreed that the named Surveyor should acquaint himself at least superficially with every wall being dealt with, and take responsibility for any decisions or actions taken by his subordinates. If you honestly feel that your position demands

[1] Eight. I thought I'd just see if you were alert.

that you should take every schedule yourself, I shall certainly not object – but I don't guarantee to meet you personally on site. Nor will I agree the payment of principal's fees for leg-men's work. There are two schools of thought about how to agree schedules of condition. One school likes to go around with its opposite number and agree everything on the spot; the other prefers to take the schedule alone, and then send it to the other surveyor (or his assistant) for comments. Then there are two schools of thought about how actually to record the condition. One school favours writing it all down; the other prefers a tape recorder. A third school (which I forgot to include in the first two) likes to take photographs, but they're no substitute for description, in my opinion. It doesn't really matter how you do it, as long as it serves its purpose, which is to help to identify any damage caused by the works.

Eventually, the schedule is reduced to writing, and this is where the word processor has really come into its own, and enormously eased the job of the party wall surveyor. In the days of mere typewriters, your opposite number used to return your painfully typed schedule (in which you'd already corrected several howlers by your typist: I had 'the terror of certain decisions' instead of 'the tenor', only today) with a few amendments, which involved re-typing and perhaps even re-paginating the whole document. Nowadays, you simply type the amendments and push a button or two for the rest. After it has gone backwards and forwards a couple of times, you will have an agreed schedule.

Now, or more probably meanwhile, you can get down to discussing the physical impact of your proposals (let's call them yours, for simplicity) upon the adjoining property. Are there special precautions needed in any respect? Is it a bank, with tremblers in the walls? Is it a restaurant, which would be closed by the Public Health authorities if dirt and dust started flying? What's the basic user: domestic or commercial? Will the structure stand what is proposed for it? Will it need underpinning? Thickening? The flues blocked off? Will the party wall need to be more firmly fixed to the adjoining premises before your building is taken down? All these and more are practical questions which form the real meat of the party wall surveyor's activities.

From time to time, though not in the general run of cases, more serious questions may arise, such as whether the wall is a party wall at all, or whether you have the right to carry out the works proposed. The first of these you have no power to deal with, since it relates to title, which is a matter for the parties and their lawyers, but your advice and judgement should be the cornerstone of their proceedings. Of course, party wall surveyors are always deciding whether a wall is a party wall or not, and that they certainly can do on the basis of clear cut evidence. Sometimes, however, there is no evidence, or it's wildly conflicting, and the parties are already at loggerheads over the ownership of the disputed piece of property. Then the surveyors are gazumped, or zugzwang[1] if you prefer it.

To illustrate this point I can tell the story of the very distinguished surveyor who came to me, the Third Surveyor, to decide just such a question. A notice had been served on his client/ Appointing Owner (you will see the reason for the alternatives in a moment) purporting to initiate work to a party wall. This owner had appointed an eminent holder of high office in the RICS, who said that it wasn't a party wall at all. After some to-ing and fro-ing he and the bowler-hatted architect who claimed to be the Building Owner's Surveyor came to me for a decision. I put my findings in a letter, not an award, saying that in my opinion it was not a party wall, so that they were not appointed under what is now Section 10, and neither was I, so that my decision was not under the Act. This had two consequences, the first of which was that nobody paid me. The second was that the architect is reported to have returned to the attack on the Adjoining Owner, saying: 'Mr Anstey says he is not a properly appointed Third Surveyor. Therefore his opinion is not binding. Therefore I say it is a party wall'. (Only if it had been, my decision that it wasn't would have been binding!) The end result, in case you're wondering, was that the Adjoining Owner threatened legal action if the Building Owner attempted to proceed under non-existent party wall rights, and the Building Owner sensibly abandoned those proposals.

As to whether the Building Owner has the right to carry out certain works or not, if you cannot decide between yourselves you can turn to the Third Surveyor for judgement, and if the Appointing Owners don't like his or your decision they can appeal. But this is to anticipate ourselves. Let us return to the run-of-the-mill case. I have dealt elsewhere with drawing up an award[2], so you can look there for the generalities. What we have just been talking about is the crucial and variable part of it: the works which the

[1]   A chess term, meaning unable to make any effective move.
[2]   See Chapter 6.

38

Building Owner wants to carry out, and the requirements he must meet if he is to be allowed to do so.

A word processor comes in handy here, too – and a photocopier. Very often, the easiest way for an Adjoining Owner's Surveyor to indicate his amendments is to make them in manuscript upon the draft award sent to him by the Building Owner's Surveyor. Then he can photocopy his amended draft and send the original back to his opposite number who, after perhaps a little more to-ing and fro-ing on certain items, simply hands it to his word processor operator who types the amendments, presses the buttons and, hey presto, a fair copy of the final award is produced. This is now photocopied as often as need be: at least two copies for the parties, and one each for the surveyors.

Sometimes, lucky you, two interests in the property will agree to be bound by the same award. Then all you have to do is change the names and addresses a little – word processor again – and there is a completely different (?) final award.

All this happens, theoretically, before any work is done which needs the authorisation of the award. Sometimes it even happens like that, but I have known awards to be finalised long after the building is up and occupied. Very often, when the two surveyors are men who know and trust each other, the official document may lag behind the works, although everything that is done affecting the Adjoining Owner will have been agreed as they went along. This is not, however, to be taken as approved practice. Technically, the Adjoining Owner is entitled to his award, and there are not a few surveyors who, whatever the standing of their opposite number or his Appointing Owner, will not allow a brick to be touched until the award has been delivered, their fees paid, and the days for appeal have run. Strictly speaking, unless the award specifically allows for those fourteen days to elapse before work may begin, the Building Owner can get cracking at once, but if there were to be an appeal after work had started, but within the days of grace, it might have unfortunate consequences. Most Third Surveyors would uphold the inclusion of a fourteen day clause. I'm sure the courts wouldn't like it if the possibility of an appeal was overlooked, either intentionally or accidentally. Note that in any case, the surveyors cannot shorten the period of notice in their award. Even if, *mirabile dictu*, everything proceeded with extreme rapidity, the earliest date on which work can start is two months (usually) after notice has been served – unless the Adjoining Owner himself consents to an earlier commencement.

Assuming once again, that we are following a normal sort of job, we may now at last let the Building Owner loose upon the party wall. We deliver his copy of the award to him (we've already extracted the Adjoining Owner's fees, so he'll be doubly anxious to be off) and, if we're prudent, specially draw his attention to any particular requirements of which he may be unaware. We will probably not specifically draw his attention to his right of appeal under section 10(17), since very rarely is such a thing even remotely justified, and it certainly isn't going to be so in our typical case. My learned friend aforementioned thinks you should tell an owner of his right to appeal, even if you don't encourage him, and that there is far more risk of a successful appeal out of time if the Owner wasn't advised fully of his rights earlier on. Other distinguished authorities support this view, and suggest writing a letter saying something like: 'You should be advised that you have a right of appeal to the County Court should you feel that there is anything in the award which should not be there, but I can assure you that I know of no reason for you to do so, since all your rights are fully protected therein'. I'm still not sure that I agree, but the weight of opinion is against me.

It is going to be important to make sure that the award is safely delivered to the hands of the Owner, and does not lie around either surveyor's office until the end of the job. Many amateurs do not realise the importance of delivery, but as the right of appeal (even if we're not going to encourage it) runs until fourteen days after delivery, it is obviously essential that those days should start to run as soon as possible after the award is signed, and although under the Arbitration Acts, time runs from when the arbitrator announces that his award is ready, it was held in *Gyle-Thompson* v *Walstreet*[1] that it didn't start until the Adjoining Owner had the thing in his possession. Finally, we impress upon the Building Owner how important it is that the contractor should be aware of his obligations under the award, and then again we sit back and wait.

What we are waiting for this time is trouble. (We won't mention the sort when the Adjoining Owner's Surveyor – the sort who wants everything signed, sealed and delivered before the first sod is turned – goes on site and finds that half the work has been done already, when the ink on the award is not yet dry.) The architect amends his plans, the engineer alters the foundations, the contractor ignores his instructions and, worst of all, the Building Owner changes

[1] See Chapter 16.

his identity[1]. All these may require renegotiation with the Adjoining Owner's Surveyor, and some of them may require service of new notices, in which case remember that a new appointment of surveyors is required[2]. New awards may be needed, but if they are only to approve variations in the works, there should be little trouble about them. Many surveyors welcome addendum awards as an opportunity substantially to enhance their fees, so they will be quite happy to enter into them[3].

Lesser sorts of trouble are quite easy to deal with. Physical damage to next-door's property is just a matter of having it put right. It would, of course, be even easier if the contractor simply got on with it and repaired it, but it seems to be a congenital failing of contractors to deny ever causing any damage to anyone. Reglazing a window therefore involves two owners, two surveyors, a contractor, a sub-contractor, an insurance adjuster, and a bill of hundreds (if you're lucky) of pounds, for something which would have cost half a crown[4] (or thereabouts) to mend.

Surprising as it may seem, many party wall jobs are carried through without causing any physical damage to the adjoining premises at all but, as I have already said, physical damage is easy to sort out. Despite the automatic denials of the contractor, responsibility is usually fairly easy to determine, and the costing of the making good is not usually very difficult. A little more trouble is frequently caused by noise, and the Building Owner's Surveyor often has to try to sort out such problems, which are not really within his remit. If he regards himself throughout the progress of the works on site as a man whose duty it is to sort out all problems between the Owners, walking a fine line between not allowing the Adjoining Owner to be put upon nor the Building Owner to be exploited, he can hardly go wrong, though he will often find himself doing more than the strict interpretation of his role would seem to require. The one essential, in my view, if he is to fulfil these wider obligations properly, is to know, and to let his Appointing Owner know, when he is acting as a party wall surveyor with power to bind and when he is acting as an adviser only. Also in my view, the Owner should take both sorts of

---

[1]   See Chapter 11.
[2]   *Gyle-Thompson*: see Chapter 14.
[3]   This is not meant as a commendation.
[4]   I originally wrote this fifteen years after decimalization, and I see no need to change it.

admonition as orders, and do what he is told, but not all Owners show such a proper sense of deference to their surveyors.

When the works are completed it is advisable, though by no means invariable, for a final inspection to take place, at which the schedule of condition is checked and any damage agreed, to be subsequently put right or paid for. Many people recommend positive action by the Building Owner's Surveyor to put this in motion, so as to secure a positive clearance from the Adjoining Owner for the Building Owner who can, barring accidents, be sure that he has now disposed of all claims from neighbours. Of course, this involves the Surveyor finding out from the Building Owner, his contractor, or his architect, when the job has actually reached the stage at which no further involvement of the neighbour's property is likely. A positive end to the job also has the advantage that the Adjoining Owner's Surveyor can put away his file for ever, either at once or after the making good, while the Building Owner's Surveyor can cross one adjoining property off his list and, when he has eventually crossed them all off, at last put in his own final bill, advise his Appointing Owner that all party wall matters are now at an end (always excepting any latent damage[1]), and consign his own file to the basement, microfilm or the dustbin. (I don't seriously recommend the last, but the tricolon is such an effective rhetorical device). Anyway, *la commedia è finita.*

* * * *

That was the situation seen from a Building Owner's Surveyor's point of view. I shall now put myself in the position of the Adjoining Owner's Surveyor.

* * * *

So there you are, sitting quietly in your office, when the phone rings. 'I'm told you know all about party walls', a voice will say. If you are me, you will reply: 'Yes'; but you, dear reader, will probably make some more modest response, nevertheless indicating that you have sufficient grasp of the subject to assist your interlocutor. 'I've

---

[1]   As the cases of *Selby* v *Whitbread* and *Brace* v *SE Regional Housing Association* make clear (see Chapter 16) a Building Owner is not relieved of his common law responsibilities, so any latent damage which emerged would still fall to his charge.

just received a . . .' – and there will be a pause while the speaker finds the form, turns it the right way up, and reads from the top of it '. . . a Party Structure Notice. What on earth is it all about? It says they're going to do works to my party wall'.

Two ways are open to you at this point. You can spend the next half-hour or, if you go to visit your Appointing Owner, two hours (since it always seems to take longer face to face) pointing out that if it is a party wall it isn't 'his', and if it is his, it isn't a party wall, and then giving a resumé of party wall law and procedure. Better far to tell him not to worry about it; you'll deal with it all; he should send the papers along to you; all he needs to do is to write to the chap who served the notice, using the acknowledgement form if one is attached, saying that he dissents and that he has appointed you. You then dictate over the phone a letter on the lines of RICS draft letter 2 (which he will get wrong, so you later send him a fair copy for him to sign) and tell him to send that to you with the papers. After that, assure him, he has nothing to worry about and nothing to do until you send him the award.

Most anxious laymen will now be quite reassured and will leave everything in your hands. Some think they know better, and will attempt to tell you how you should make things difficult for the Building Owner, preventing him altogether from carrying out his schemes, or delaying him as long as possible. Once again two choices are before you. You can decline to act further, and throw the whole thing back at him, or you can take what I regard as the professional approach and (I mean this in all seriousness, though you may find it surprising) ignore him. You simply do your duty as a party wall surveyor[1] and refuse to impede the Building Owner or his surveyor, unless they should try to do anything improper. A certain Adjoining Owner once became very wrathful at what he regarded as his surveyor's wilful refusal to act as he should, constantly disobeying orders to be obstructive, and generally going his own sweet way. He rang up the RICS in high dudgeon, and complained bitterly. 'Never mind,' said the soothing young lady in the Building Surveyors Divisional Office, 'I'll put you in touch with a really nice party wall surveyor, who'll sort out all your problems. His name's John Anstey.'

'John Anstey!' spluttered the chap on the other end of the phone. 'That's the *!*! I've got acting for me!'

[1] See above.

Typically, however, a short word of explanation will be all that's needed to make the situation clear to your anxious enquirer, and three days later (if the Owner has used first class post) the papers will be on your desk. Your first duty is to see that your Owner's interests are protected, so you must assure yourself that he has dissented and that you have been properly appointed. It doesn't matter too much whether he has dissented if it really was a notice under Sections 3 or 6, but not everybody has the sense to use the RICS forms of notice, and some others can be quite confusing. However, it is always helpful if dissent is explicitly expressed, since then everybody knows what is going on, and even who the parties and their respective surveyors are.

While you are checking the notice, you will obviously see whether the Building Owner or his surveyor has filled it in properly. Very often he won't have done so, and as it is in everybody's interests that the formalities should be correct, you should at once write pointing out any deficiencies, while stating that you have no objection to getting on with the mechanics of the affair, while the errors are being corrected and notices re-served. I have had some clients who have sought to make the most effective use of defective notices by not telling the opposition until the last possible moment of their error – say, when they're just about to start work. I deplore this behaviour, and say so, unless the Building Owner is also trying to get away with some skulduggery, and is therefore fully deserving of a little tit for tat. I prefer to communicate with the other side at once and, as you don't want to get on bad terms with the Building Owner's Surveyor at the outset, this letter has to be written tactfully. The reason that it is in your Appointing Owner's interests to get everything straight is that he is going to be given certain protection by the award. If the proceedings are a nullity because of a defect in the notice, then so will be the award and the benefits it affords.

I regret to say that not all Building Owners' Surveyors recognize that this is meant to be helpful. If you ring them up and tell them about defects in the notice they have been known to accuse you of obstruction, whereas in fact you are attempting to assist them. Do not allow the curmudgeonly attitude of a few to deter you from acting as a proper party wall surveyor – and always feel free to tell me if I've got something wrong in a notice. I once told Eric Roe's Appointing Owners that I proposed to demolish their building. He had great fun putting me right.

If everything is in order on the notice and the dissent, you may care to send a copy of your letter of appointment to the Building

Owner's Surveyor, and ask to see his, particularly if he has signed the notices, when you will want to see his authority to do so, for the reason set out above.

Now you must agree upon a Third Surveyor. This is as much your duty as his, so if he has not suggested anyone so far, you may send him a list of names to choose from[1], usually three. His agreement in writing upon one of them completes this exercise. A schedule of condition of your Appointing Owner's premises is usually one of the next steps. This is more for the Building Owner's protection, in fact, but Adjoining Owners like to see it being done. It makes them feel that someone is taking an interest in them, and they think that the schedule is for their protection – which to some extent it is.

Meanwhile, you will be considering the proposed works and, in particular, whether they are permitted under the Act. It may be that you will need to point out that a wall they propose to use is not, in your opinion, a party wall, or that they will be making use of works carried out by your Owner, and so liable to pay a contribution under section 11(11)[2]. You will be deciding whether there are structural details which go beyond your competence as a surveyor. Let me point out that straightforward questions should not be too much for you, or you shouldn't have accepted the appointment in the first place. However, if there are complicated engineering questions, your Appointing Owner will need expert advice. The engineer's fee will have to be covered in the award, so you must seek your opposite number's agreement that such advice is reasonably required, and that he will award payment of fees sufficient to cover the engineer's as well as your own.

You may have enough competence to tell whether any rights of light issues arise – or other easements. If so, don't attempt to cover them in the award[3], even if you don't call in an independent consultant to deal with them.

Read the draft award carefully, when the Building Owner's Surveyor sends it to you. Check that the works covered therein are those declared on the notice. Ensure that your Appointing Owner is protected against damage, and against noisy works at unnecessarily inconvenient times. Check that you have an unfettered right of entry to the Building Owner's premises to see that everything is being done in accordance with the award.

[1] See Chapter 1.
[2] See Chapter 10.
[3] See Chapter 14.

As soon as you have agreed all the documentation, and signed it, publish it to your Appointing Owner. This is his one legal chance to interfere with your actions, and he must be given it. Don't encourage him to appeal, though, but do remember that some people think that you certainly should advise him of his right. You may have nominated a number of visits during the course of the works as part of the justification of your fee. Do look in to see that all is well, even if you are not beset with constant cries for help. You will probably have to explain to your Appointing Owner that the award only regulates work to the party wall, and not elsewhere, and that the noise he is complaining of comes from well over on the other side of the site. Nonetheless, it is probably no bad thing to try to keep general noise levels down in the interests of neighbourliness, and you may be lucky enough to have a Building Owner's Surveyor who thinks the same.

From time to time, damage may occur. Impress on your Appointing Owner that he should tell you about it at once. If he happens to have next door the one foreman in the country who believes in putting right any little bits of damage without argument, you may never need to do any more about it, but it is far more likely that you will have to call in your opposite number to agree upon responsibility and making good. At all costs, try to stop your Owner from putting it right and removing the evidence before any of the professionals involved have seen it.

Try to find out when the works are coming to an end – you'll be extremely lucky if anyone bothers to tell you – and arrange to make a final inspection of your Owner's premises. It's much more helpful if any damage can be noted and discussed before the contractor leaves the job, even if it is going to be the Building Owner's responsibility towards the Adjoining Owner in the first place. There's no reason why you shouldn't help him to recover from the people who actually did the damage and, who knows, it may even be more convenient to have the contractor put the damage right himself, particularly if it's external, such as mortar droppings, blocked drains or cracked roof coverings.

If a lot of damage has occurred, you may be justified in asking for an additional fee for dealing with it, and you may even need an addendum award, although an exchange of letters is usually all that is required. When the damage is all put right, and the final payments have been made, you can sit back and wait for the phone to ring again.

Chapter 5

Notice

There are two aspects to the matter of giving notice: how to do it, and how much to give. There is an easy answer to the first part: use the RICS form. This isn't, however, what you might call the correct answer, to which I shall at once turn.

There is no statutory form, not the RICS one and certainly not the RIBA one, on which notice must be given. You will find that some people, semi-professionals rather than amateurs or real professionals, demand to receive a 'proper' notice, if you send them anything except a printed form. If your only wish is to appease them, then use a printed form. If not, then draw their attention to the words of the Act which are, in section 3 at least (and the words in section 1 and section 6 are like unto them) '. . . a building owner shall serve on any adjoining owner a notice . . . stating a) the name and address of the building owner; b) the nature and particulars of the proposed work . . .' and a lot of detail about special foundations again. Obsessed with special foundations, the authors of the Act were. Whether, therefore, you write a letter or use a form, those particulars must be included. You must also give the date when it is intended to start work.

In the case of a notice under section 6 you must, as I have remarked elsewhere, also include plans and sections, which is extraordinary, the extraordinariness lying in the fact that you aren't required to include them in a notice under section 3 unless special foundations (again!) are involved. (Why, I wonder, and do not intend to provide an answer, does the notice of works under section 2 get a section of its own, 3, while one under section 6 has to be content with a sub-section, (5)?) It cannot be wrong, and is certainly helpful to the recipient, to provide plans with your notice whatever it concerns, and almost the first request an Adjoining Owner's Surveyor will make is to receive some, if they haven't already been sent to him.

Included in the information with your section 6 notice must be plans and sections showing the site and the depth to which you propose to excavate. It is not enough to say: pile depth to be decided on site. Funnily enough, no-one is likely to quibble if you change the intended depth, even quite drastically, and later substitute 50 foot piles for 20 foot ones, but they are very likely to reject your notice as inadequate if it mentions no depth at all.

I am coming to periods of notice shortly, but it should be noted at this stage that there are minima and maxima. I wouldn't be at all surprised if a court were to rule that a notice that purported to name a starting date outside the limits was completely void, and could not be validated simply by the amendment of the date. You must give the date at which you expect to start work; it must fall within the prescribed limits; and if, as so often happens, you have been instructed that the job is starting next week, while two months' notice is needed, you can only beg the Adjoining Owner's indulgence – not, be it noted, his surveyor's. In order to avoid silly errors of putting a date in for starting, and then forgetting to sign and send the notice for a couple of days, so that the starting date is now less than two months away, in my office we usually write 'as soon as notice has run', which cannot be incorrect.

Hold on, I hear you cry. Who is serving the notice? Is it an Owner or his surveyor? The answer is that (see above) the Building Owner must give notice, but his hand is usually being held by someone else. When I first began specialising in party walls, it was almost invariable for the Building Owner himself actually to sign the notices, even if he hardly knew what he was signing. In the face of considerable opposition at first, I have gradually made it acceptable for the Building Owner's Surveyor, who understands far better what is needed in the notice, and who frequently did all but the signing in the past, to sign and serve the notices himself, provided he is armed with a suitable letter of authority from his principal, because in this case he is acting as the agent of the Owner, not as his appointed surveyor. This is now so much the generally accepted practice that the RICS publish a draft letter for giving that authority.

An odd little problem that crops up sometimes is finding out who the Building Owner is. (It's often hard to find out who the Adjoining Owner is, and we'll come to that shortly.) Under the complicated financial arrangements which seem to prevail these days, and which I don't pretend to understand, the chap who is actually going to carry out the building often doesn't have a legal interest (though he may have an equitable interest) in the site until the day before the works begin – if then – but the Building Owner can't assign, in my opinion, the benefit of a notice which he has served on behalf of the incoming developer. The man who serves the notice must be the one who is going to do the building works (see the definition of building owner) and he must be an owner within the definition given in the same section. Sometimes developers don't tell you that they don't actually own the site – it's wounding to their *amour propre*, and they always talk as if they 'own' all the sites they're concerned with. They are also inclined not to inform you which of their subsidiaries is going to be the nominal owner, and you tend to find that out when you send them the award, and they send it back and ask you to change the name in it!

Always ask, at the outset, who has the legal ownership of the site and, if appropriate, which subsidiary is going to be involved. The Act does specifically recognize as an owner someone with a contract to purchase or an agreement for lease, so the incoming owner will have an interest before completion. If the result of these enquiries is that the 'wrong' person owns the site at present, then the only solution I can offer is the one which I adopt: to serve in the name of the present owner and, as soon as the 'new' owner has his interest, ask the Adjoining Owner to waive the waiting period of a new notice.

Counsel has pointed out that the definition of owner 'includes' various categories. That means that it is not necessarily limited to those specifically mentioned, and the courts might well hold, therefore, that a building owner in possession of the site was the 'Building Owner' in the eyes of the Act. It may then be sufficient for such an owner to serve notice on his own. A purchaser under contract who hasn't yet entered into actual possession most certainly qualifies in this way. This doesn't, however, remove the necessity for finding out which name the developer is operating under.

Under the LBA, the actual service of the notice was covered by a section of whose existence many people were ignorant, namely 124, which also dealt with the problem of unknown Adjoining Owners. Now that the Act is much shorter, section 15 which deals with service is likely to be better known. Notice has to be sent by post in a prepaid letter, or delivered to the residence, place of business, or registered office, according to who is being served. If you can't find out who owns or occupies the premises you can simply address your notice to 'the owner' or 'the occupier', naming the premises in question and posting it as before, or delivering it, and if you can't find anyone on the premises to hand it to, you must have it fixed 'to a conspicuous part of the premises'. It is so easy to comply that there can rarely be any excuse for failure to serve notice. In addition, I always accompany notices with a letter asking the recipient to let me know if he holds from anyone, or if anyone holds from him. It's not infallible, however. I was once six months into a job before the borough council, whom I fondly believed to be the freeholders, informed me that they were only head leaseholders. Very occasionally, you may find that the same person or company owns more than one of the properties which adjoin the Building Owner's site. You need only serve one notice on that Adjoining Owner, though you must specify therein all of his properties which are going to be affected.

It's preferable and, I think, creates a better atmosphere, if you can address the Adjoining Owner by name, so don't automatically take the easy way out and serve all your notices on 'the owner' or 'the occupier'. Try to identify as many of them as possible. It's always a good idea to start by asking your client – as you haven't served notice yet, he's still your client, not your Appointing Owner – what he knows about the ownership of next door. Often he will have been in contact with the surrounding properties for some reason or other, such as trying to buy them, and can let you know quite a lot about them. You can go and read the name plates on the door, if you're dealing with office buildings, and you can consult the local Kelly's Directory. You can even ring the bell and ask.

The point of this, of course, is that notice must be given to all owners and, says the Act, 'owner includes (a) a person in receipt of . . . the whole or part of the rents or profits . . . ; (b) a person in possession of land, otherwise than as a mortgagee or as a tenant from year to year or for lesser term or as a tenant at will; (c) a purchaser of an interest . . . under a contract . . . or under an agreement for a lease . . . '. There can be almost as many 'owners' in a building as there are coffee beans in Brazil. As with Building Owners, these may be people with not very obvious equitable interests, either as purchasers under a contract or lessees under an agreement for lease. One vexed question, not yet satisfactorily settled, is whether a holding-over tenant has an interest which comes within the definition. Some surveyors, quoting an analogous decision in a valuation case, hold that he does. Others, applying logic, say that he doesn't. Be warned that he might. Several surveyors have suggested that more could be said about this subject, but the truth is that we need a good leading case or two to determine whether these equitable interests qualify their holders as owners, building or adjoining. A reliable informant says that the answer as to whether a holding-over tenant is an Owner is that immortal response: yes and no. True holding-over arises from periodical tenancies or from the effluxion of a fixed term tenancy. The first gives rise to a similar periodic holding, and the second to a tenancy from year to year: neither of these qualifies as ownership. In the case of an expired business tenancy, however, the tenant can go on occupying virtually for ever, unless the tenancy is brought to an end by one of the means envisaged by the Landlord and Tenant Act. This latter kind of holding-over tenant probably therefore is an Owner.

Virtually no council tenants are Owners, and I'm sure that you don't need to give notice to mortgagees. My own practice is not to rely upon the Building Owner's doubtful standing when I am serving notice on his behalf, and to assume that a tenant in occupation may well rank as an Owner, whatever his status. In the latter case it is probably better to serve in haste and repent at leisure.

Then there is the bicycle shed against Dolphin Square problem. (Dolphin Square used to be the biggest block of flats in Europe.) Upon how many of the owners do you have to serve notice if your proposed building affects only a small piece of wall? The question quite often seriously arises in blocks of offices where, say, a top floor is being added to a block which has a party wall with another building in multi-occupation. Certainly you must include the freeholder (and any long leaseholders) and the occupier immediately adjoining the works, but what about those lower down (or sometimes further up) the same wall? It is my opinion that, strictly speaking, unless their demise includes the part of the wall being worked on, they are not entitled to notice. However, if their bit of wall might be affected by settlement or any other disturbance transmitted through the wall, either upwards or downwards, it would probably be wise to include them in the service. There are other ways of dealing with Adjoining Owners besides serving notice, if you think that one is not legally required. You can write a friendly, neighbourly letter saying what you intend to do, and you can even take a schedule of condition without being governed by the Act.

There are a number of counter notices referred to in the Act. Occasionally, people even serve them. Sometimes, even the right people. The Act requires the Owner to serve the counter notice, and his surveyor can only do so if specifically authorised. The term can probably be extended to cover all formal letters of response, whether they are so described by the Act or not. The first to be so mentioned, though not a counter notice as such, is a consent in writing to a proposal to erect a party wall or party fence wall at joint expense, under section 1(3)[1].

Consent in writing is always necessary for a proposal to use reinforced concrete foundations on an Adjoining Owner's land, and section 3(3)(a) makes it clear that the procedures of section 10 are not necessary if the Adjoining Owner has formally expressed his approval.

The counter notice proper follows immediately after, in section 4. This lists two positive kinds of dissent, if you see what I mean. They don't actually dissent from the proposed works, but they ask for more to be added unto them. If the Building Owner is proposing to carry out work to a party structure, the Adjoining Owner can require him to build in chimney breasts, piers, and the like, for his convenience, while if he is consenting to special foundations, he can ask for them to be deeper or stronger so that he can use them.

No counter counter notice is required. Silence to a section 4 counter notice has the same effect as silence to a section 3 notice: it produces deemed dissent after fourteen days.

No notice is necessary if works have to be carried out under a Dangerous Structure notice, (section 3(3)(b)), while for gaining access to adjoining premises, although fourteen days is normally necessary, in an emergency only as much notice 'as may be reasonably practicable' needs to be given.

Although there are periods of notice mentioned in section 10, they are of a different nature, and I shall leave them to another, shorter, chapter[2]. I must, however, deal with how long a period of notice is needed in the sections I have covered: I think that a table is probably the simplest and clearest way to show this, but observe that not all notices require the same kind of response.

Section	Works	Period of Notice
1(2)	Building a party wall	1 month
1(5)	Building a wall on his own land	1 month

[1] See Chapter 3.
[2] See Appendix III.

Section	Works	Period of Notice
1(6)	Placing foundations on Adjoining Owners' land	More than 1 month and less than 12 months
3	Any works to a party fence wall, special foundations, or any works to a party structure	2 months

Note: all works notified under section 3 must be begun within 12 months

Section	Works	Period of Notice
4(2)	Counter notice re special foundations or other matters	1 month
5	Consent to a notice under section 3	14 days
6(5)	Building within 3 or 6 metres	More than 1 month and less than 12 months
6(7)	Consent to 6(3)	14 days
8(4)	Entering adjoining premises	14 days

Chapter 6

Preparation of an Award

It is a lot easier nowadays to prepare an award than it used to be. There are basically two forms in common use, one of them more common than the other, so we'll deal with the latter first. It begins:

AWARD
IN THE MATTER OF
THE PARTY WALL etc. ACT 1996

TO ALL TO WHOM THESE PRESENTS SHALL COME we S. Lake, FRICS of 13, St Bartholomew's Street, EC1 in the County of London, and S. Hopgood, FRICS of 31, Quoin Street, St Bartholomew's, EC1 in the County of London

SEND GREETING

WHEREAS M. D'Souza and Company of such and such an address hereinafter called the Building Owners are the owners of premises known as somewhere or other.

AND WHEREAS Y. Groenvynck and Company of another address hereinafter called the Adjoining Owners are the owners of premises known as something else.

AND WHEREAS the Building Owners desire to exercise the rights given to them under the Party Wall etc. Act, 1996, notice whereof was served on the Adjoining Owners on or about the 16th day of May 1997.

AND WHEREAS a dispute has been deemed to have arisen between the Building Owners and the Adjoining Owners.

AND WHEREAS the Building Owners have appointed the said S. Lake to act as their Surveyor and the Adjoining Owners have appointed the said S. Hopgood to act as their Surveyor.

AND WHEREAS the said two Surveyors have selected Sir Edgar Horne, PPRICS of Another World as Third Surveyor and agree that in the event of his being unable to act and their not jointly deciding upon a substitute another Third Surveyor shall be appointed by the Appointing Officer.

This last phrase is an old bone of contention. The Act certainly calls for that gentleman to make the appointment if the two Surveyors can't agree, but many people, among whom I am included, think that if the two Surveyors agree to put the choice in someone else's hands, there is no reason why they should not. If they don't agree, see above. As explained in Chapter 1, the Superintending Architect of the GLC used to hold a list of suitable Third Surveyors, but under the new dispensation each Borough Architect (or similar) will have the power to appoint in default of agreement. It is not clear whether they will each have their own list, or share a common one. In the circumstances, some surveyors who have hitherto been reluctant to divert the choice to the President of the RICS may be more inclined to do so.

The other sort starts rather more prosaically:

Whereas M. D'Souza and Company of such and such an address (hereinafter referred to as the Building Owners) owners of the premises known as such and such did on the 29th day of February One Thousand Nine Hundred and Ninety Seven serve upon Y. Groenvynck and Company (hereinafter referred to as the Adjoining Owners) owners within the meaning of the Act of the adjoining premises known as such and such, notice of their intention to exercise the rights given to them under the Party Wall etc. Act, 1996, Section 6, by executing works as more particularly defined in the notice.

It, too, then deals with the appointment of surveyors, and goes on something like this:

Now we, being two of the three Surveyors so appointed, having inspected the said premises, DO HEREBY AWARD AND DETERMINE as follows:

1. (a) That such and such address is an adjoining building standing close or adjacent to the boundary.
   (b) That the building is sufficient for the present purposes of the Adjoining Owners.
   (c) That the condition of the fourth floor of the building is as described in the schedule of condition dated such and such attached hereto and forming part of this award.
   (d) That drawing nos. such and such attached hereto and signed by us the said two Surveyors form part of this award.

These are really only the preambles, and the meat of the award follows in which the works are set out, together with the manner of their execution.

Many examples of this latter type in fuller form can be found, but particularly readily in the RICS booklet, *Party Wall Legislation and Procedure*, which is based on The Pyramus and Thisbe Club's[1] approved draft award. I will assume that you are going to buy, or have bought, the RICS publication, and will not produce a sample here. I shall concentrate on the two aspects of producing a final document which are, firstly, producing a satisfactory draft and, secondly, getting it agreed.

Before I do that, however, let me just mention the school of thought which holds that surveyors are simple, straightforward practical men, not complicated devious chaps like lawyers, and that their awards should therefore eschew all flowery pseudo-legal language, and read thus:

On 11th October, M. D'Souza ('the Building Owner') served a notice on Y. Groenvynck ('the Adjoining Owner') under Section 46(1)(e), about the building at 100, Whiteacre Street, EC1.

Y. Groenvynck dissented from the notice and appointed as his Surveyor S. Lake of 13, St Bartholomew's Street, EC1.

M. D'Souza then appointed as his Surveyor S. Hopgood of 31, Quoin Street, EC1.

The two Surveyors selected as Third Surveyor Sir E. Horne of Another World, and so on.

I must admit that this style has a certain naive charm, but it hasn't caught on yet, and even its most enthusiastic advocate doesn't

---

[1] See Appendix V.

seem always to practise what he preaches. I don't think an award in this form would be any less effective in fact or in law.

I will therefore now deal with the practical aspects of producing an award, and leave you to choose whichever style of presentation you prefer. I do urge you, however, especially if you are a beginner, to follow a reliable draft at least the first few times you try to prepare an award. It's all too easy to miss out something essential if you try to write your own version from scratch.

The first page or so will deal with 'recitals', that is to say the sort of information I have illustrated above, and it should be a straightforward record of fact: the names and addresses of the owners, the names of their surveyors; the third surveyor; the addresses of the properties concerned (not necessarily the same as the addresses of the owners in commercial cases, although usually so in domestic ones); the date of notice; the type of notice (party structure, three metre or six metre) and/or the sections under which it was served.

The next thing to do is to state the basic nature of the structure/s you're dealing with. Is it a party wall, or are there two independent buildings? State which. Say whether the wall serves the needs of the Adjoining Owner adequately: this will help to explain any apportionment of costs. Record the taking of a schedule of condition if one has been taken (and if not, why not?). Formally incorporate it in the award, and do the same for any drawings you propose to attach to the award.

A word about drawings. If you had signed as many drawings as I have in the two days immediately preceding my writing these words, you'd be astonished that I still have the power, let alone the inclination, to lift the pen. (I should point out that the whole of this work is hand written and the original manuscript will be on sale for a fabulous sum after publication.) (Note to the second edition. No acceptable offer has yet been received for this precious MS. Well, let's be truthful: no offer at all. My publisher has suggested auctioning it at the next Pyramus and Thisbe Club Christmas Lunch.) (Note to the completely new and revised edition: the revisions are all in manuscript on a photocopy of the third edition.) Most awards have too many drawings attached. In the old days, by which I suppose I really mean pre-1939, most awards were accompanied by 'party wall drawings' showing precisely, and often showing only, the relationship between the Building Owner's and the Adjoining Owner's buildings, in plan and section on one or two sheets. Nowadays, a combination of architect's, engineer's and the odd party wall drawing are used, frequently unselectively, so that bundles of ten or more drawings may be involved. Not only does this make the award document ridiculously bulky, but it also makes the lay Appointing Owner far less likely or able to appreciate what is involved.

My advice, therefore, is to limit the number of drawings to be attached to the award to the bare minimum. That does not mean that the Adjoining Owner's Surveyor should not possess a full set, but only that they are not all necessary in the final document. You may, as implied above, still need to produce a drawing specifically for the award, or to have it produced by the architects. There may be abutment or flashing details which are inadequately covered elsewhere, and which are of more import and interest to the Adjoining Owner and his Surveyor than the make of lift or the type of ironmongery.

It is very important at this juncture to differentiate between the works that the Building Owner wishes to do, and those that he must do, for the protection of the Adjoining Owner, if he implements the former. This was the nub of *Marchant* v *Capital and Counties*[1], but the gist of the Court of Appeal's decision was that all works referred to in the award which may be necessary for the good of the Adjoining Owner must be carried out by the Building Owner, once he decides to proceed with his works, and that in the event of any ambiguity (and, I would submit, even in the face of a plain contrary meaning) in the wording of the award, it will be construed in favour of the Adjoining Owner. You must be careful, therefore, to put into the clause concerning works which the Building Owner wants to do all those things for which he needs the power of the Act, as no right to do more than is stated is likely to be susceptible to subsequent inference. It is usual, indeed, to add that no material deviation from the stated works shall be permitted without express agreement. It is also worth stating that the Building Owner is under no obligation to carry out his own works. You won't be thanked for binding him to proceed with a major development when his financial circumstances are causing him to hesitate before starting.

Now you can turn to those things which are a condition of your being allowed to do what you (or the Building Owner) want. These are fairly standard, and are listed in the RICS draft award, but there may obviously be specific requirements for a particular job: a

---

[1] For a full discussion on this case, see Chapter 16.

particular problem of support; attention to tremblers in the wall of a bank; filters for air conditioners; or the shuttering off of part of the adjoining premises in order to allow the demolition of the party wall. It is usual to specify at this point whether access to the Adjoining Owner's property is necessary for carrying out the works, or even that it is to be avoided. Section 8 will give you the right of access if it is needed[1].

The rights of access of the two surveyors must also be covered. It is usual to give the Adjoining Owner's Surveyor a much more free hand than the Building Owner's Surveyor. There is usually no good reason why the former should not be allowed on to the site at any time when work is going on, to see that his Appointing Owner's rights are being respected, and it is equally reasonable that the latter should have to give notice (or make an appointment) if he wants to come on to occupied premises to inspect something.

Hours of working are often specified – or at least of noisy working. This can lead to acrimonious discussion, especially in mixed company, by which I do not mean the growing band of lady (or do they prefer 'women'?) building surveyors. It is easy enough, provided you are prepared to put up with restrictions at all, to agree to limit working to suit one class of Adjoining Owner – office, shop or domestic – but when all three are closely entwined there is no hour of the day or night when one of them will not want you to be silent. On the whole, the courts are more generous in allowing hours of noisy working than Adjoining Owners' Surveyors are, so you could always threaten recourse to them, if you are the Building Owner's Surveyor. However you settle the matter, here's the place in the award to do so.

It is usual to say (but I think unnecessary) that the works should be in accordance with any other statutory requirements and the Act[2]. It is more necessary to say that the works must proceed without undue delay, and to put in a time limit for their completion. An award is not a perpetual licence to a Building Owner to interfere with the property of his neighbours. It may be necessary, and it is certainly usual, to reserve the right for the surveyors to make further awards as necessary, although in my opinion the duty placed upon the surveyors by Section 10(10) to 'settle by award any

---

[1] See Chapter 9.
[2] Sometimes even planning consent is included.

matter (a) which is connected with any work to which this Act relates, and (b) which is in dispute . . .' clearly gives them such power, whether the first award specifically says so or not. Fees for the Adjoining Owner's surveyor are usually, but not quite invariably, set down in the award[1], and some surveyors refuse to sign or hand over the award until they see the colour of the Building Owner's money. Personally, I regard this as unprofessional and would only do it if I had been jilted more than once by the same man. Technically, it might be correct for the Building Owner's Surveyor's fees to be laid down in the award, and the responsibility for them placed upon the appropriate owner (which might well be the Building Owner!) but it is seldom, if ever, done[2].

The last effective clause usually found in an award was much debated by the RICS Working Party before we resolved upon its inclusion. This virtually repeats the gist of section 9, and points out that an award does not override easements of light or others in a party wall. For that reason, its mention is unnecessary, but we decided in favour because the Owner who gets the award is probably not familiar with section 9, and this spelling out reassures the layman that his rights in such respects are unaffected.

You should now have a draft award which needs no amending, but it is a rare bird indeed which returns to the ark without some additional feathers stuck in by the other surveyor. I don't think I actually said that draft awards are usually drawn up by the Building Owner's Surveyor. Well they are, but not invariably . . . If you, a knowledgeable, experienced, Adjoining Owner's party wall Surveyor (which you will be by the time you've waded through all this, even if you weren't already) find yourself dealing with an innocent architect who has suddenly been called upon to grapple with the intricacies of the Act as a Building Owner's Surveyor, it will often be a positive kindness to both of you to relieve him of the attempt to write his first award from first principles[3], and send him one of your own.

Let us assume the more usual circumstances. As the Building Owner's Surveyor you are certainly better placed to describe the intended works and it is only reasonable that most of the burden of producing an award should fall upon you. You now send it to your

---

[1]   More about fees in Chapter 7.
[2]   Noel Coward.
[3]   Which I warned you against a few pages ago.

opposite number. Theoretically, he has ten days to act upon it[1], but he may well need some urging to get on with it: his owner isn't champing at the bit, waiting to get on with the works. Theoretically, if he doesn't reply within ten days after a written request to do so, the first surveyor can proceed *ex parte*, but this is a course which is usually only taken as a last resort. Instead, the Building Owner's Surveyor writes increasingly urgent letters as his Appointing Owner writes him increasingly demanding ones – demanding to know when he's going to get signed awards.

If you are the Adjoining Owner's Surveyor it is your duty to respond promptly to the receipt of a draft award. Apart from anything else, you are putting your Appointing Owner at risk of an *ex parte* award, and so you should deal with any points of disagreement in the draft and send it back. It is often helpful to discuss these on the telephone, so that what you are sending back are, in effect, agreed amendments, and they should preferably be written in different coloured ink on the draft so that the other surveyor can immediately identify them. This process should normally only take one exchange of documents and one telephone call. Very often, you may prefer a slightly different method of wording some clause or other, but it's not really productive to be pedantic about things like that. As long as principles are unaffected, let it go.

The same goes for the Building Owner's Surveyor when he gets the award back. If the other chap's amendments don't really affect the basic working of the award, why bother to quibble? Have the thing fair copied, and made up into a nice document with its accompanying drawing (that's just a pious hope for the singular) and schedule.

When it comes to the final document, we have to deal with the date and the signatures. You wouldn't think that people could get this wrong, but they do. The first signatory should not date the document, which is not effective until the second man signs: so the latter dates it. Oh, by the way: I always refuse to sign a page with no effective part of the document on it. A page with just a date and signatures looks pretty silly on its own, and is in theory more easily misapplied than one which is actually part of the award itself.

The named surveyor should, of course, actually sign in the presence of the person who is going to add his name as witness. I

---

[1]   See Appendix III.

am meticulous about this, and even stop signing if the witness is called out of the room for any reason – such as going to fetch a pen! But I'll bet some people aren't so scrupulous. I have even – occasionally – received 'witnessed' awards lacking the Surveyor's signature. I am advised that the witnessing is not, strictly speaking, legally necessary, but it can be highly desirable and, if it's going to be done at all, it should be done properly.

The witness should be of legal age, and should give their personal address, which is not that of the office, unless they happen to be a principal of the firm. I usually write back to such offenders congratulating them on having a living-in secretary, or on having made some junior a partner. Contrary to what I thought, it is perfectly proper for a wife to witness a husband's signature on an award.

Finally, the surveyor should sign the schedule of condition and all the drawings (hence my complaint a few pages ago) and perhaps date them. I do not think that they need to be witnessed.

Really finally, the completed award should be promptly despatched to the respective owners (section 10(14)), so that the period for appeal can begin to run as soon as possible after the award is complete, since both parties are bound by the award if no appeal is made. That was really finally, until the second edition came along. In order to avoid too much alteration to the existing text, I put another couple of paragraphs on to the end of this chapter, and they still hold good for the national Act.

It is, of course, perfectly possible and often desirable to have more than one award on a job. Quite often, the Building Owner will not have details of the superstructure available when he wants to get on with the foundations. It will probably cost him more in fees, but save him even more in time (and therefore money), if he asks his surveyor to produce what may be called a 'Foundation Award', to be followed in due course by a 'Superstructure Award'. Sometimes even these two are not enough, and may be preceded by a 'Demolition Award'. Very often, this last is a legal fiction, since the Building Owner does not need its sanction to make his activities legal, but it helps to establish the relationship between the parties and produces an agreed schedule of condition which has all the air of being legally binding, so that I would not discourage the use of such 'Awards'. I would, however, utter a mild word of caution against relying too heavily upon one if faced with an Adjoining Owner intent upon exploiting every loophole.

I have often been asked when an award comes to the end of its effectiveness, and before *Marchant* v *Capital and Counties*[1], I would have said that it ceased to apply as soon as all making good was completed at the end of the works covered in the award. The Court of Appeal made a ruling which implies that in some circumstances the award can run indefinitely. I think that it was a bad ruling – and the wrong one on the facts, as it happens – and that in the majority of cases the award will still die with the end of the building contract next door or, at the latest, soon after. Don't forget that the Adjoining Owner will still have his common-law rights if some unforeseen catastrophe should strike him at a later date.

---

[1] See Chapter 16.

Chapter 7

Fees

How on earth can you write about fees, when they're going to have changed their value as soon as a book is published? You can't, of course, but you can offer general guidance.

Circumstances are completely different for surveyors depending upon whether they're acting for Building Owners or Adjoining Owners. I never take a job on for a Building Owner except on a time basis. I will give an estimate, if I can, and I will certainly quote the hourly rates which I will charge, but I will not tie myself to a fixed sum. You cannot possibly tell, when a job begins, whether the contractor will make for a smooth and happy relationship with all the neighbours, or whether you will constantly have to be dashing down to the site to clear up after damage – metaphorically speaking.

I charge different rates for different grades of staff: about two-thirds of my rate for a junior partner, half for a senior assistant, and one-third for juniors. It should be remembered, however, that in a firm as specialised as mine even juniors are extremely knowledgeable and experienced in party wall matters, so these proportions may not necessarily be appropriate for others.

Travelling time can be a bone of contention. For a central London firm dealing with central London jobs, it hardly matters, and they will quite frequently visit two or three jobs in one outing. There are provincial firms (by which I mean in the Home Counties, as well as further afield) who take on party wall work in London and want to be paid for three hours travelling time on each site inspection as well as being paid at metropolitan rates for their time spent on site. Doubtless, under the new dispensation, there will be London firms seeking to take on work in distant parts of the country, and not only wanting to be paid their usual metropolitan rates but also for their travelling time and costs. Unless it is a very specialist matter requiring the sort of top class expertise for which it is always right and proper to pay extra, I do not think that such charges can be justified. More than one such claim has been taken to the Third

Surveyor. If offered work in distant parts for Adjoining Owners, surveyors should either fit their visits in with other business in the area, or else pass the work on to someone else in the first place. If neither of these courses is open to them, then they should charge either moderately or not at all for travelling. It's quite different for Building Owners, of course. They're going to foot the bill, so that if they choose to engage an expensive expert from distant parts, that is their prerogative.

You should not charge principal's fees for doing leg-men's work. It is not always easy to decide what constitutes work demanding a partner's time and attention, and what can safely be left to juniors, but the effort must be made in all but one-man-bands. I repeat that it is perfectly acceptable for the vast bulk of the work to be done by capable assistants, and it is in everyone's interest that it should be so, not least that of the man who is footing the bills, provided that the assistants are charged for at appropriate rates.

At least the Building Owner's Surveyor's fee charging is comparatively simple, even if his position as agent, adviser or arbitrator[1] is not always clearly defined: at the end of the job he tots up the hours and bills his client/Appointing Owner accordingly. What's more, the Building Owner has complete control over whom he appoints, at least at the outset (although if he changes his opinion about his surveyor, he can't change his appointment). If he wants to appoint the man in the moon and pay his travelling expenses to monthly site meetings, that's up to him. The Adjoining Owner's Surveyor, however, is thrust upon him, and that's when the Building Owner's Surveyor has to protect his Appointing Owner by resisting claims for extortionate sums.

The position of the Adjoining Owner's Surveyor is far more complicated. It is only reasonable that he should be asked to calculate an overall fee for the job as a whole, given a fairly normal progression from notice to completion. By the time he inserts the figure in the award, a lot of the work will already have been done, and the scope of the work will certainly be clear. He can always protect himself against unforeseen complications by careful wording of the award[2]. However, a certain amount of guesswork has to be done, and some people are rather notorious for the high level of their guesses. This is not fair on the Building Owner, nor is it a professional attitude to

[1] See Appendix IV.
[2] See the last few pages of Chapter 4.

one's job. Make a reasonable estimate, and hope for swings as well as roundabouts or vice versa.

Slightly more problematical is the question of how to charge for an Adjoining Owner's unreasonableness. If he constantly drags you down to the site, wrongly alleging that work to the party wall has started or that damage has been caused, should such visits be charged to the Building Owner? In equity, they certainly should not, but there's little hope of recovering fees for them from your Appointing Owner. The sort who call you out at the least provocation are just the sort who will strongly resist the suggestion that they should pay for it. I don't pretend it is a perfect solution, but I suggest that you should send them a note of your fees, but not by way of a VAT account, telling them that you will send such an account when the fee is paid. You may be able to square it with your conscience to charge half the fee to the Building Owner, if the Adjoining Owner does not pay you.

Then there is the small works question, on which I have written at length elsewhere[1]. It is just not fair that the owner of a suburban terraced house, anxious to carry out a small alteration to his property which affects both his neighbours, should have to pay West End fees to three party wall surveyors. The fees very soon begin to wag the works.

A former employee of mine was appalled recently to be told by an Adjoining Owner's Surveyor, working for a well known and formerly respected firm, that his fee would be a minimum of £1,000 (or thereabouts) for a job, of the details of which he knew nothing. My friend protested that while he would be perfectly happy to agree an award with a fee of £2,000 if it was justified, he was not prepared to agree to £1,000 if the proper figure was £500. You may be as disturbed as I was to learn that the initial reaction to this was to say: 'Well that's our minimum, and if you won't pay it we'll send the papers back to the Adjoining Owners'. I am happy to say that, backed by my enthusiastic endorsement, the Building Owner's Surveyor succeeded in making the other side see reason.

I know that it costs as much (if not more) for the surveyor to travel from his office to a distant residential job as it does to stroll round to a big commercial development, but you must temper the wind to the shorn lamb: take a loss on the job, regard it as useful experience, and help the little man to a swift and efficient end to his works. You may even be laying up for yourself treasure in Heaven.

[1] See Chapter 1.

66

Chapter 8

Going to the Third Surveyor

Suppose you cannot agree upon the basic terms of an award. It doesn't happen very often, but it's not unknown. Suppose you can't agree the Adjoining Owner's Surveyor's fee. This often happens but is usually compromised. Suppose you can't agree about damage and remedial works. This happens quite frequently. Do you go to law about it? Certainly not. Do you yell and scream abuse at each other? Yes, I'm sorry to say, but it doesn't get you anywhere. Do you go to the Third Surveyor? You certainly should, and with less diffidence than is often shown. There is nothing to be ashamed about in asking a respected fellow professional to settle an honest difference of opinion, and you should surely have no hesitation in asking the same chap to tell some pig-headed opponent just where he's going wrong.

Before you actually refer a dispute to the Third Surveyor comes one of those rare moments when you actually consult your Appointing Owner. The reason for this is that he may be called upon to bear the costs of the reference, and he will definitely be forced to put up with the delay while the matter is decided – as to which, more later. He may well, therefore, decide to submit to some imposition – a restriction on working hours, an inordinate fee – rather than risk the other consequences. Once your owner, knowing the issues, decides to proceed, you write to your chosen arbiter.

You have been told elsewhere[1] that he may not want to have heard of his selection heretofore, and this will probably be the first he knows of the matter. Your first letter should therefore acquaint him very briefly and simply with the outlines of the dispute, and ask him if he is willing to act. It may be helpful to send him at this stage evidence of both surveyors' selection of him, whether in a semi-official form or else simply by an exchange of letters. A signed award, if the disagreement comes after the award, is usually good evidence, since it will probably record his selection.

---

[1] See Chapter 1.

From here on, the procedure rather depends on the man chosen. However, a typical case might go as follows. On receipt of your letter, the Third Surveyor asks both surveyors to supply evidence of their appointment, copies of notices, and any documents so far agreed. He will then call both surveyors before him and try to get at the root of their disagreement. Sometimes this will be all that is needed, and the intervention of a clear-headed outsider will either result in a compromise, or else reveal to one party where he is wrong. This often produces no fee for the Third Surveyor, but enhances his reputation and probably makes him feel good inside.

More often, a problem which is not immediately soluble presents itself. Having heard the first thoughts of the two contestants, the arbitrator/umpire/Third Surveyor (for he is certainly one of those, probably two, and maybe all three) will want to see the scene of the crime. He will arrange access, with both or neither of the two, not with just one of them, and will ask each of them to submit a formal statement of his case, giving the other a copy and an opportunity to comment. It is important that justice should be seen to be done, but it can be dangerous to allow comments on the comments, and comments on those. Things can get out of hand – I've had a submission to me as Third Surveyor on which I ought to have been able to write a decision ages ago, but I'm writing this chapter instead, because neither party will let a single letter to me go by without a counterblast from the other. My practice, until recently, was to require both surveyors to submit their case in full to me, copy to each other, and then to allow each of them one riposte. This, I eventually realized, put the more prompt man at a disadvantage, because his opponent received the case, and drafted his original submission accordingly. He then waited for the opponent's riposte, and replied to that. Nowadays, I direct that each should send two copies of their submission to me, and only when I have both do I send the copies out to the other side.

The LBA used to allow the Third Surveyor fourteen days to make his award. General informed opinion had it that this must mean fourteen days after he was in possession of all the evidence he needed: after all it frequently takes that length of time for a busy arbiter – and they're likely to be the best sort – to fit in a visit to the site. Recognizing the impossibility of laying down a timetable for the Third Surveyor, especially when delays are usually caused by the failure of the other two surveyors to make their submissions quickly, the new Act does not specify when the award must be made: merely that the Third Surveyor must get on and make it. When he has written it out, usually with the same sort of preambles as the customary two-man form, he leaves it unsigned and undated, and informs the two surveyors of the fact that it is ready, and may be taken up on payment of his fee. He tells them what the total is, and it is then up to them and their owners whether they each pay half of it, or one of them pays the whole.

Within the award itself, probably as the very last clause, will be the directions as to eventual responsibility for the Third Surveyor's fees. Quite often one party will be held liable to pay all the fees and it may well not be that one who was so anxious to collect the award that he quickly paid in full – and sometimes the fees may be split equally or unequally between Building Owner and Adjoining Owner. There is a tendency to regard all disputes as the Building Owner's fault, but one must guard against always making him pay.

When he has received his total fees, the Third Surveyor signs (witnessed) and dates the two copies (or perhaps even three, so that he retains an original) and, regardless of who paid, sends both awards out either to the parties or their surveyors, who must forthwith send the originals on to their Appointing Owners in accordance with Section 10(14). The surveyors might add useful comments on the Third Surveyor's Award, including the possibility of appeal if they think that the award is clearly wrong: not just disagreeing with their opinion.

How should you, a young, inexperienced surveyor, who has refused to be browbeaten by your older opposite number, who tells you that he's done more awards than you've had hot dinners, present your case to the Third Surveyor? First of all, remember that you probably agreed to his selection (unless early argument forced reference to the Appointing Officer[1] even for this element of the equation), so he's not necessarily a potential opponent, nor an ogre. If you've chosen well, me or someone like me, your youth will certainly not be held against you – provided that you don't come in chewing gum with a fag behind your ear, and as long as you call me sir.

Don't weary the Third Surveyor with irrelevant history. Stick to the points at issue, and try to keep any personal animosity (for it must be admitted that some does occasionally arise: in Donald Ensom's waiting room once, I threatened to punch the nose of an

[1]   See Chapters 1 and 6.

architect who later became a good and friendly client) out of your remarks and behaviour. Observe the same strictures in the written presentation of your case. Make sure that all the items in dispute are dealt with: the Third Surveyor won't be pleased to be asked to make a further award because you forgot something. Keep your comments on the other side's representations brief, and make sure that they're clearly related to the originals, using his numbering of paragraphs, if there was any, or making clear by the use of words what exactly it is that you're rebutting.

Politely direct the Third Surveyor's attention to any legal matters which you think may assist your case: leading decisions; the wording of certain sections of the Act; this book? Don't regard losing a dispute, or even not wholly winning, as being a slight on your professional reputation. It may be, of course, but in that case all the reading in the world isn't going to help you, because to lose in that way will show that you're not fit to do the job in the first place. Happily, that sort of person is not likely to be reading this book. An honest loss can be an education, or just one more weight in the scale of experience. Finally, really to encourage you, I should point out that each time I have lost a party wall case in the courts my reputation seems to have increased greatly. Do try to win, though, or you shouldn't be there.

Chapter 9

Access to Next Door

Many people think that you have a right to go onto someone else's land to get at your own building. Indeed, I have known objections to planning applications along those lines: 'If permission is granted I will be unable to paint my windows/render my wall/clean my gutters!' In earlier editions of this book, I wrote that 'although there has been talk about an Act of Parliament to give such a right (which, like most Acts brought in to correct what is thought to be some injustice, would probably turn out to lead to some very unjust situations on the other side of the coin – or boundary) there is no such general right at present.' As you probably know, the Access To Neighbouring Land Act, 1992 has now been passed, and my prediction of some unjust results has also come true. For a full exposition of that Act see the College of Estate Management's booklet under that title, written by a well known expert. It was held in *Bond* v *Nottingham Corporation*[1] that you could enter an Adjoining Owner's land to preserve your right of support, if that owner's inactivity was allowing it to decay; however, many people feel that this case was wrongly decided, or not of general application, but in any event unsafe to rely on. I am not of their number, but I feel that I should warn you of this body of opinion. Of course, you can acquire all sorts of rights to go on to other people's land, and even to pick their cabbages, by prescription or grant. Outside these rare occurrences, however, your neighbour's land is his own, even if you try to do the work without setting foot on his actual soil, suspended from sky hooks, since *cuius est solus eius est usque ad coelos et ad inferos* which, being translated, means that if he owns the ground then he owns everything from the centre of the earth up to the heavens, always barring government intervention in the matter of minerals, overflying, et cetera.

However, the rights given under the Access Act are strictly for works of maintenance and repair, not for any development or

---

[1]   See Chapter 16.

extension. The position under party wall legislation is completely different from that under common law or the Access To Neighbouring Land Act. Under the Party Wall Act, you do indeed have a right to go on to your neighbour's land, and in a big way. Let me first of all explain what the Act says, and then point out some of the snags.

Section 8(1) says that 'A building owner . . . may during usual working hours enter . . . any premises . . . for executing any work in pursuance of this Act . . .' which looks fairly straightforward. If you are doing any work under an award[1], because there has been a difference between the owners which has been settled by the surveyors, then quite obviously your rights are clear. If the award envisages your need to go next door to erect scaffolding or to excavate, or to take down the wall, or to shutter off some part of the Adjoining Owner's building, then section 8 gives you clear power to do so. Furthermore, it goes on to say at 8(2) that you may break down the door with a policeman. (I must point out that this graphic version of this sub-section, which now has quite wide currency, was mine originally and, I think, enables you to remember the gist of it.) You have to give fourteen days notice of your intention, or as much as possible in an emergency.

It may occur to some of you that there are times when it is an advantage to have a party wall instead of one of your own. If you want to go next door to do the work, which gives you the better chance, nay, the right? Quite correct: the former. So as long as there's no overriding reason why you need total control of the wall, if next door want to treat it as a party wall, why not let them? It's an even better bet (although *Marchant* v *Capital and Counties*[2] may just have changed this) than you might think, because awards do not run with the land, and so no decision by two surveyors to treat a wall as a party wall (or not, for that matter) can be binding on any surveyors that follow them, and therefore when it suited a later surveyor to argue that the wall was not party, he could do so. Remember, ownership of the wall is a matter of title, and surveyors are not empowered to decide ownership or boundaries by their position under the Act, if these questions are seriously disputed between the owners. In practice, the surveyors are usually deciding, from the evidence, which category walls come into, and on whose land they are standing, and there is usually no argument. If they

[1]   See Chapter 6.
[2]   See Chapter 16.

deliberately made a wrong decision, it would not be legal, and would be readily appealed against by either owner. In any case, this is not to be taken as encouragement deliberately to argue either way as it suits, but only to point out that if both sides are happy to treat a wall in a certain way, argument may be unnecessary.

I see two difficulties in the operation of section 8. If you are carrying out work which does not require an award, under section 1, for example, or even by express consent to a section 3 notice, it may come as a considerable shock to the Adjoining Owner to receive your fourteen days' notice of intent to enter, and he may make some difficulty about it. However, the words are clear: the Building Owner 'may enter . . . any premises for . . . executing . . . any work in pursuance . . . of this Act'. It doesn't even say that it has to be necessary – not at this point – and it might be argued that mere convenience would justify doing the work from the Adjoining Owner's side. It is to be hoped that responsible surveyors would not make an award allowing unnecessary access causing unreasonable inconvenience, but the permission is certainly very wide. It gets a little narrower in the last few words of sub-section (1) of section 8, where the word 'necessary' does appear, and this is where the second difficulty comes in.

The Building Owner may '. . . take any other action necessary for that purpose'. 'Any other action' is so broad in its scope that 'necessary' only narrows it down a little. Take a not altogether hypothetical case. A party wall, agreed to be such because it stands on a boundary of ownership, doubles as a retaining wall for an uphill garden, and the external wall of a downhill building. Either owner has an absolute right to take it down and rebuild it, but whichever of them does so is going to cause an awful lot of disturbance to his neighbour, while it is hardly thinkable that the work can be carried out without going on to the land of the Adjoining Owner. If the uphill garden is subsiding, the owner can only maintain the support by going downhill and rebuilding, so he must be allowed into the next-door building. If the downhill property owner wants to rebuild he may find great difficulty in doing so if he cannot go into next-door's garden and cut back some of the soil while he excavates the old wall and constructs the new.

Either of the parties to such an arrangement is going to be unhappy when whichever happens to be the Building Owner tells the other of his plans, and they will probably argue at length as to whether what he proposes is lawful. When forced to concede the existence of section 8 the Adjoining Owner will rely on 'necessary', and demand that the Building Owner prove his necessity. When all three surveyors have adjudicated on the subject, one party may well (I told you this wasn't entirely hypothetical) appeal the eminently sound award of the distinguished Third Surveyor.

Let us consider an even more straightforward – or is it? – case. As you have read[1], under section 1(5) a Building Owner may build a wall on his own land at the line of junction without objection from the Adjoining Owner, but must serve notice of his intention. As there is no provision for objection, there can be no appointment of surveyors and no award. He can just get on with it, including putting foundations on next-door's land. Now section 8 says nothing about work under an award, or appointment of surveyors. It simply says that 'A building owner . . . may . . . enter . . . and may execute any work in pursuance of this Act'. Well, section 1(5) is in 'this Act', so in my opinion our Building Owner is entitled to the benefit of section 8. But must he go on to next-door's land to do the construction works?

Certainly it will be easier for him if he can scaffold the building externally, and get on with other jobs inside, and not to mention the fact that the wall will look so much nicer. Actually, it pays to mention this fact to next door, even if outside the Act, because it is they who will be looking at the wall after it's built, and they should prefer to see a neater wall. If, however, there were a building next door, built right up to the line of junction, you obviously couldn't go into it in order to erect a fair-faced wall, nor would you want to, since nobody would be going to see its face, fair or otherwise. Therefore, is it necessary to go on to the Adjoining Owner's land if there is no building there?

My opinion is that the necessity must be a matter of judgement for the surveyors, and I would also argue that section 10 covers the settlement of any argument between the owners. Remember that the section starts by saying: 'Where a dispute arises . . .'. 'Dispute' is not a term of art, and does not mean only a formal dissent under section 1, 3, or 6, and the clause goes on to say 'in respect of any matter connected with any work to which this Act relates', so that if a Building Owner served notice of entry under section 8, for whatever purpose, and an Adjoining Owner disputed it, their difference should be settled under section 10[2].

---

[1]   In Chapter 3.
[2]   See Chapter 1.

Chapter 10

Who Pays for What?

It is a common fallacy that the Building Owner is bound by the Act to pay the Adjoining Owner's Surveyor's fees. The Act makes no such categorical statement. At section 10(13) it says that the reasonable costs of 'making or obtaining an award' together with the cost of reasonable supervision of the works shall be paid according to the award of the surveyors. In fact, this means that in ninety-nine cases out of a hundred the Building Owner does pay, but only because that is what the surveyors decide.

It is of course reasonable that any costs directly arising from the Building Owner's intention to build should fall upon him, and therefore the reasonable fees of the surveyor necessarily appointed by the Adjoining Owner, both to prepare the award and to keep an eye on the property while the works are being carried out, should form a natural extension of those costs. However, some argument has arisen as to what is a necessary part of 'making or obtaining' that award. Quite apart from discussion as to the reasonableness of fees in general[1] there are frequent disagreements over the incidence of solicitors' fees and those of consulting engineers.

Solicitors' fees are easily dealt with. There is no need for a solicitor anywhere in the proper operation of the Act, and therefore just because an Adjoining Owner, on receiving a notice, has consulted his solicitor, there is no justification for charging his fees to the Building Owner. However, if the Building Owner has attempted to proceed without due regard for the procedural niceties, so that the services of a solicitor have been necessary to get him to go through the proper motions then, in my view, the fees for those services have been properly incurred in 'obtaining' an award, and the surveyors should not hesitate to award their payment.

Engineers' fees are a little more tricky – and a little more frequently paid – but in essence they follow the same principle. If

---

[1] See Chapter 7.

the Adjoining Owner's Surveyor has called in an engineer to advise whether the bricks should be red or yellow, or whether the underpinning should be done in bays of three feet or one metre, then the engineers' fees should not fall on the Building Owner, but if the works are of such complexity that they fall outside the competence of a reasonably able building surveyor, then those making the award are likely to agree that a consultant's fees are a necessary charge. It is therefore beholden, in my opinion, upon anyone undertaking work as a party wall surveyor[1] to make sure that he is competent to deal with the technical matters involved. If he is not, he should refuse the appointment. Alas for vanity, this good advice is not heeded often enough in more fields than party wall surveying but, oh joy!, how much work comes thereby to expert witnesses.

There are certain direct instructions as to responsibility for costs of construction in what one might call the prime moving sections: 1, 2, and 6. In 1(3)(b) the cryptic remark is made that the cost of building a new party wall or party fence wall 'shall be from time to time defrayed by the two owners in such proportion as has regard to the use made or to be made of the wall by . . .' and goes on to add that such defraying shall also respect 'the cost of labour and materials prevailing at the time when that use is made . . .'. This becomes less cryptic when read in conjunction with 11(11) and 11 (7)[2], and what it means is that when Mr White builds the wall, all Mr Black needs is a garden wall, so he pays half the cost of one. Mr White, however needs a four storey warehouse wall[3] and he pays for the rest. If, later, Mr Black wants to use more than a two metre high garden wall, he can be called upon to pay a fair, current market, contribution.

Section 2 is a little more subtle in handing out responsibility, which is why you should always carefully observe which sub-section is quoted in a notice. The big difference is between 2(2)(a) and (b) or (e), as you will see when you reach the discussion of section 11 which follows in a page or so. Under section 6 there is a plain direction that the Building Owner is responsible for the cost of any necessary underpinning (or strengthening or safeguarding) of the Adjoining Owner's foundations.

It goes without saying that the Building Owner is responsible for any damage that is done by the works carried out under the

---

[1] And see Chapter 1 for the necessary qualifications.
[2] See later in this chapter.
[3] The astute may notice a subtle reference to a real case.

award, but that responsibility is rather more firmly fixed than it is under common law. Not only is he made directly and specifically liable for any damage done under certain sections, to which I shall very shortly come, but also the award firmly states, in almost every case, that he shall immediately make good any damage occasioned to the structure or decorations of the Adjoining Owner's premises – or words to that effect[1]. The Adjoining Owner cannot then be fobbed off by being referred to the management contractor, to the main contractor, to the sub-contractor, to the sub-contractor's insurers, or to the insurer's loss adjusters. That now only happens to the Building Owner's Surveyor, who finds himself pursued by all those people for having prejudiced their position by agreeing a figure of damages with the Adjoining Owner's Surveyor. Bully for him, I say. He has acted in accordance with the law and the award, and he has settled the matter in dispute between the Owners. How the Building Owner settles it on his side and where he fixes the ultimate responsibility is up to him, but the man who has suffered has been properly and promptly indemnified.

An award is not, however, a let-out for a Building Owner if the Adjoining Owner's Surveyor has approved a method of working which then proves to be inadequate to protect his Appointing Owner. The case of *Brace* v *South-East Regional Housing Association Ltd,* 1984[2], although not a London Building Act case, makes this clear, as does section 6(10). The Building Owner is always responsible for the results of his actions.

Since it is apparent that almost any party wall work is likely to risk causing damage, it is curious that the Act singles out certain operations for specifically making the Building Owner liable. No doubt some day someone really intent on a legal battle will claim that inclusion of some sub-sections must be deemed to exclude all others, but surveyors are generally more sensible. It is worth noting, however, just which sub-sections do include an express liability, and they are: 1(7); 2(2)(a), (e), (f), (g), (h) and (j); and 7(2).

The first time that compensation is mentioned is in section 1(7) where any damage from placing footings on the land of an Adjoining Owner is to be made good to that Owner and any occupier. I've never experienced such a case, but there it is. (It has been pointed out to me that some gardeners have been known to

[1] IYRU rule 40.1 (but probably about to be deleted).
[2] See Chapter 16 for further discussion of this case.

wax very wrath if their flower beds are not reinstated.) Then comes section 2 and while you can carry out fantastic acts of demolition and rebuilding under sub-sections (b) to (d) without causing any damage, apparently, possibly because the works are for the joint benefit of Building and Adjoining Owners, when you get to (e) you are liable to cause the damage and to pay for it until you reach (j), but you can do (k) (l) (m) and (n) without penalty. I don't propose to repeat here what those sub-sections are, because you can find them elsewhere[1], but I do think it strange that the Act does not say simply: any damage to the adjoining premises shall be made good at the cost of whichever party the surveyors shall decide. There is a kind of logic to who's in, who's out, but since some of the outs are likely to have to come in, it all seems rather pointless.

You may be surprised to hear that there is no specific liability for repair should you have cause to break down the door with a policeman (section 8)[2].

There is a whole section of the Act, section 11, devoted simply to 'Expenses'. This deals with the payment for actual building works, and is much simplified from the LBA. It is quite logical and simply summed up: if the work is for the sole benefit of the Building Owner then he pays, but if the Adjoining Owner derives some benefit, then he contributes his fair share.

Sub-section (1) says that the Building Owner always pays, except where the rest of the section says otherwise. If the work is of repair to the party wall, the expense is apportioned according to the use made of the wall and the responsibility for the defect.

The provisions of 11(7) are a little more complicated. If the Building Owner seeks to reduce the height of an existing wall (under 2(2)(m)) the Adjoining Owner can require him to keep it up by paying an appropriate share of the modern cost of its construction. Section 2(2)(e) is the big one, of course. That's when the whole party wall may be pulled down leaving you exposed to the cold night air[3]. You certainly will have suffered inconvenience as you are shuttered off from the party wall, and then rejoined to it. You will have been deprived of the use of a certain amount of space for a certain period, which should be fairly easy to value, but you will also have been inconvenienced in a more general way:

[1] See Chapter 3.
[2] See Chapter 9.
[3] Or, more probably, other measures adopted: see Chapter 3.

cramped, dirty; workmen in and out. Section 11(6) says that the Adjoining Owner is to be paid a 'fair allowance in respect of disturbance and inconvenience'. I wish I could offer concrete guidance on how to assess such disturbance. I can only suggest that it may be helpful to agree the easily established costs as quickly as possible and then, perhaps, agree a percentage addition to reflect the less easily assessable losses.

Frankly, there is no way I can think of to make these provisions exciting to read about. They are hardly ever brought into discussion, since they mostly state the obvious. I shall simply plough on, since this is meant to be a comprehensive work, but if you're not already asleep, why not save this bit of the book until you want a nap.

Sub-section (9) says that if the Adjoining Owner demands that the Building Owner has to carry out some additional works, then he has to pay for what he asked for. That's reasonable isn't it?[1] Similarly reasonable is sub-section (10) which makes the Building Owner refund to the Adjoining Owner any additional costs to which the latter is later put because of the existence of reinforced foundations.

Sub-section (11) says that payment must be in current money values. In other words, when the Building Owner discovers that it's going to cost him £2,000 to enclose on next-door's wall, it's no good saying that it would only have cost the (now) Adjoining Owner £500 five years ago. The sum to be refunded is the present cost. The same must be true of other payments, for example for extra costs caused by special foundations under 11(10). One way out of this is to agree the cost of doing the work now, and for the Building Owner to pay it to the Adjoining Owner. The latter can do what he wants with it: he could buy the entire recorded oeuvre of Louis Armstrong or Dietrich Fischer Dieskau (approximately equal, I should think); or he can invest it and realise it when he comes to do the work. The Adjoining Owner should have no objection to this way of dealing with the matter, but he cannot compel the Building Owner to do it: the latter can quite properly refrain from paying until the work is about to be done. You may be confused about who is the Building Owner and who is the Adjoining Owner: I certainly am. The answer is that, in these questions, they have swapped sides, and you can probably call each of them either.

[1]   Johnny Stanley: *floruit c.* 1955.

Who, by the way, is the Building Owner from whom this sum is to be recovered? Is he the chap who did the work (and where is he now?) or the present freeholder or the tenant on a full repairing lease? Sue someone, and let me know the answer: I think it's the present freeholder.

Finally, we come to sub-section (11) itself. Under the LBA this was the notorious section 56(4) and gave rise to a lot of confusion because it referred to a wall raised under 'this Act'. In strict legal terms that appeared to exclude the 1894 one. You apparently therefore didn't have to pay to make additional use of a wall raised before 1930, even though you would have had to do so in 1929. The same was seemingly also true of a wall raised without going through the procedures of the Act – which may not have been entirely unjust. These anomalies are avoided in the new Act, which simply says that when an Adjoining Owner later makes use of work paid for by the former Building Owner, he has to pay the appropriate share of the current cost of that work.

In case it's not obvious how this situation arises, let me give an example. Two semi-detached houses stand side by side. (They'd look pretty silly if they didn't). The owner of the left-hand property puts in a loft extension, raising the party wall to enclose it and he pays all the cost. Ten years later, his neighbour in the right-hand house decides that he would like a loft extension. He has a right to use the already raised wall, since it is party, but he has to pay his share of the modern cost of construction. Almost certainly, the recipient of the payment will be the current freeholder of next door.

'Security for expenses' is a little-used provision of the Act (section 12), sometimes abused, and occasionally not employed when it would have been a good idea to do so. It operates in two directions: first, if the Adjoining Owner fears that the Building Owner's operations may leave him unstable (financially or structurally) he can ask the Building Owner to put up a sum of money, and this is quite often done when the latter only has an address abroad; second, if the Adjoining Owner requires the Building Owner to carry out work for which the former may have to pay all or part of the cost, the latter may ask for security. That does not mean that you should always request security against possible damage, but undoubtedly the fear of damage prompts a large proportion of the few requests for security which are made.

I was once involved in yet another case in which the judge went to extraordinary lengths to make the words of the LBA mean something other than what any sensible man (i.e. me) would understand them to mean. (The worst case of this, in my opinion, is *Leadbetter*[1].) An Adjoining Owner demanded (with the encouragement of his surveyor) security for expenses. It became quite clear during the course of the hearing that the surveyor didn't really understand the method of working proposed; that his Appointing Owners had been needlessly alarmed; and that what they were really after was security for damages which, as I've just remarked above, is not what I think this section is intended to cover.

The judge appeared to have a much better grasp of the building techniques involved than did the Adjoining Owner's Surveyor. (I may say that I only understood them because my assistants had carefully explained them to me.) He said that if he had any discretion in the matter he would have found for the Building Owner, but he didn't find any words in the LBA expressly giving him that option. He was of the opinion that he could fix only the amount of security: but that, in my opinion, clearly gave him discretion to settle upon the sum of a penny or nothing. That equals discretion to make an award or not at all.

However, I repeat, he didn't see it that way and awarded a moderate sum of security, but left each side to bear their own costs – which spoke for itself. It was small satisfaction to my side that they had offered a better settlement than that before the hearing. I still think that the judge was wrong. Fortunately, whereas under the LBA the only method of settling arguments about security for expenses was through the courts, the new Act gives all the procedures of section 10, that is to say the three surveyors, for use in the first instance, with the County Court available for an appeal if the parties are not content to accept the surveyors' determination.

This is one (or two, depending on how you look at it) of the reasons why changes of ownership during the progress of works, or during the period of notice, may make it necessary either for the proceedings to begin *de novo*, or for the parties to be bound by what has gone before[2].

Note that it is the Owners who have to ask for security, not the surveyors. I'm not sure why this change of responsibility occurs: indeed, the surveyors are more likely to know whether security is needed, since they will not only be aware of the structural risks

---

[1]   See Chapter 16.
[2]   For a detailed discussion of this point see Chapter 11.

which may be being taken, but may also have met the particular developer before and know that it will prove difficult to extract reparation if things do go wrong.

We may be sure, however, that the surveyors will be well to the fore in the background to start with, and possibly later even in the foreground, because the most common way of dealing with security money is to put it on deposit in the name of the appropriate party, usually the Building Owner, and provide that it shall only be disbursed on the instructions of any two of the three surveyors. In many cases, nothing requires to be paid out and the whole sum, together with accumulated interest, is returned to the original depositor. Arguments have been advanced that the interest should be shared, but they can be rejected, since the non-depositor has no right to anything save his security, and if he has needed no indemnification, then all the money reverts to its provider.

Finally, if you're still awake, or if the exciting provisions of sections 11 and 12 have re-awoken you, we come to the last two sections of what used to be Part VI. Extraordinarily, the surveyors now step back into action. Section 13 requires the Building Owner to submit a formal account for any work to which the Adjoining Owner is required to contribute, within two months of completion of the works in question, and says that if the Owners disagree about any rates, apportionment or other like matters 'a dispute shall be deemed to have arisen' – and we all know who settles disputes.

The effective last section of all (because there are still some technical sections to come[1]) is not the most exciting. It merely states that until the Adjoining Owner has paid up his share, the Building Owner retains sole ownership of the works in question.

[1] See Chapters 5 and 13.

Chapter 11

Change of Ownership

This is one of those matters where you have to take my word for it. I know of no really useful legal guidance on the subject, and so I have had to work out my own ideas on the points in issue. We had intended to have a lecture on the question once, at The Pyramus & Thisbe Club, but somehow it was metamorphosed into a talk on Turkish Baths instead.

If the Building Owner changes during the course of works, before or after an award has been drawn up, then, in my opinion, the whole proceedings have to start *de novo*. The Act is very personal in its application, and I can see no authority therein for the transfer of rights by a vendor Building Owner to his successor in title. When drawing up an award, the two surveyors may be influenced in the way clauses are worded by their knowledge – or lack of it – of the track record of the developers: whether they always honour their obligations under an award and (which is not always so easy) whether they see that the contractors do; whether the Adjoining Owner's Surveyors' fees are promptly paid; whether damage is quickly put right or paid for; whether noisy works are carefully controlled. All these factors may influence the rigidity of an award. Furthermore, the whole emphasis of the Act is a personal one: you do not appoint a firm, you appoint a surveyor[1]; an award does not bind land or sites, it binds Owners. I conclude, therefore, that you cannot pass the benefit of an award to an incoming Owner. He may be quite unknown to the Adjoining Owner and his surveyor or, often worse, well known.

If you consider the question of security for expenses[2] under section 12 you will realise that an Adjoining Owner may readily allow a particular Building Owner to start work, even of a sort which puts the former's building at considerable risk, without asking for

[1]   See Chapter 1.
[2]   See Chapter 10.

any security, relying upon the latter's reputation for fair dealing and financial soundness, whereas if the property is disposed of to a man (or company) of altogether less exalted reputation, the Adjoining Owner may want very ample security indeed. It would therefore surely be inequitable that the benefits of section 12 should be denied him: the negotiations must start afresh with the service of new notice in the new name. However, the Building Owner who served the original notice cannot escape the consequences of that service by disposing of the property. Any damage done or fees incurred will be his liability although very often the kindly purchaser will relieve him of it. *Selby* v *Whitbread*[1] is a case which bears on this point.

There is the problem of the change of ownership which has been known about and anticipated all along, to which I have alluded when dealing with the service of the notice[2]. An intending purchaser is to be the developer, and wants to get everything in order and prepared for starting before he completes his purchase, but until he has a contract to purchase he does not (according to my present view of the law) come within the Act's definition of an Owner. It is hard on him, I admit, if he has to wait two months after contract, when all the details could have been tied up in an award long before. The solution which I used to advance was for both parties, vendor and purchaser, to join in service of the notice. I am not sure about the legality of this procedure, but it is certainly equitable, since Adjoining Owners know from the outset who they are really going to be dealing with, and yet notice is served, albeit jointly, well in advance by the then owner of the legal interest.

The extension of this system and theory has only just this moment occurred to me, but I now realise that it can be used to deal – at least partly – with the purchaser who buys during the progress of a job. As soon as the vendor knows that he has the deal as good as concluded, he serves new notices in the joint names of himself and the purchaser, so that the new negotiations can be got on with and the new awards produced while the writ of the old awards still runs. On completion, the new awards supersede the old, and there is no awkward hiatus. Of course, in most cases additional fees will be incurred, but in comparison with the cost of delay they'll be cheap at the price. However, the majority opinion seems

[1]   See Chapter 16.
[2]   See Chapter 5.

to be against me on this point, and the alternative solution is to serve in the present Owner's name, proceed as far as possible and, when the new owner is properly entitled so to be called, serve fresh notices and beg the Adjoining Owners to waive the period of notice.

The position of an Adjoining Owner who disposes of or acquires an interest is more complicated and yet, I think, more obvious. It is obviously inequitable (the more alert among you will have noticed that I keep stressing this question of equity: that is because I think that that is the approach which the courts would take, in the absence of express legislation on the point) for a Building Owner who has done everything properly to be frustrated by the sale of an Adjoining Owner's property. An Adjoining Owner who was absolutely determined to thwart or, at the very least, postpone for as long as possible the intended works of a Building Owner could move the property around between subsidiary companies or friends and relations, forcing the service of fresh notices every time, if that were a legal manoeuvre.

No, that cannot be right. The Act gives a Building Owner certain rights, and it must be intended that, provided he fulfils his duties properly, he should not be improperly impeded in the exercise of them.

What, then, is the position of an adjoining ownership which changes its identity? In my opinion, a vendor or lessor is bound fully to disclose to any purchaser or lessee the existence of party wall negotiations and the extent to which they have proceeded. The latter will be bound by those proceedings, as far as they have gone to date. If notice has been served, the new Adjoining Owner needs no new notice. If a surveyor has been appointed, that surveyor must carry on acting for the new Owner. If an award has been made, then the incoming Owner is bound by that award just as much as if he had been the person on whom notice was originally served. In my opinion, these guidelines apply equally, whether an interest is disposed of from, say, one freeholder to another, or whether a subsidiary interest is created from, say, a head-lessee to a sub-lessee. In fact, there should be no serious difficulties on this side of the wall, because it is hard to believe that a sale or lease could be completed more quickly than a party wall award, provided that the surveyors knew that there was some urgency about the matter. All it needs is for anyone who is thinking of getting rid of their holding to tell their appointed surveyor, because it will be much tidier if the award is in existence and the new owner takes possession with full knowledge of it.

Unfortunately, in all the excitement of making a financial killing in the disposal, the Owner frequently forgets to tell his appointed surveyor at all – or his successor in title. The first that either party knows about it is when the surveyor pops in to see how things are going, and sees a strange face, while the strange face wonders who this is barging in as if he owns the place. I suppose that this innocent purchaser might have a right of action against the vendor, if he feels that he has not bought what he bargained for, but I remain convinced that he is firmly fettered by the proceedings already under way.

One little problem that I don't suppose I would have thought of if it hadn't actually happened to me, is the question of who gets any compensation under section 11, and at what moment does the compensation become payable? When the award is signed, or when the additional use is actually made? Suppose the money is paid with the award, but the disposal takes place before the use is made. Should the first Owner pay the money over to the second Owner? In the actual case with which I was concerned, I was in possession of the cheque for the section 11 compensation when the change of ownership took place. Neither party actually knew about it, since I had negotiated the matter as a natural part of my duties as the Adjoining Owner's Surveyor, and was going to break the glad news to him when I signed and delivered the award. At that very moment, I was informed of the sale. My solution was to ask the vendor whether he had conveyed the property with the full benefit and burden of the party wall proceedings to the purchaser. He replied that he had and so, without revealing why I had asked the question, I paid the money over to the delighted new Owner.

If I am to sum up this chapter, I think I can do so by saying that when the Building Owner changes, so does everything else, but when the Adjoining Owner changes, everything goes on as if he hadn't. At least, that's my view of it.

Chapter 12

An Appeal

An appeal is a disaster. A reference to the Third Surveyor is not. The reason for this dichotomy is that the latter is subject to implicit time restrictions, whereas the former is not. It can fairly be said that one of the functions of the Act is to keep negotiations between owners proceeding at a reasonable pace, but naturally it stops short of imposing time limits on the courts, and that's where an appeal is dealt with.

Very, very occasionally an appeal is justified by the fact that an award goes beyond the powers of the surveyors: *Gyle-Thompson*[1] was such a case. Then, faced by an award which allows a Building Owner to do something to which he has no right, the Adjoining Owner has no option but to ask the courts to protect him. But the wheels of the law grind very slowly indeed, and the poor Building Owner may find himself unable to get on with his work at all while the matter drags through the inexorable legal processes.

What can be done to avoid such an awful fate? First of all, of course, you should try never to go beyond your powers in an award, and to see that both Owners' rights are constantly in your mind when drawing one up. That's at least one good reason for following a reliable model, as I have recommended elsewhere[2]. You are less likely to go astray if you are on the rails of good guidance than if you are rambling down an unmarked path. Secondly, and I'm sure there are those who will disagree with me here, you should not draw your Appointing Owner's attention too forcibly to his right to appeal. I was certainly right about disagreement. I had no sooner drafted this paragraph than I was jumped on by a distinguished *confrère* who said that you must make very sure that your Appointing Owner knows of his rights. He felt that the uncertainty of whether an appeal was allowable outside the fourteen days[3] could be

---

[1] See Chapter 16.
[2] See Chapter 6.
[3] See *Gyle-Thompson*, Chapter 16.

avoided if an Owner had been advised of his rights and failed (or declined) to exercise them. Of course, if you have lost an argument in front of the Third Surveyor, who has agreed with your opposite number, and you think that you were so right that the decision against you is not just unfavourable, but wrong, then no doubt you not only have a duty to inform your Appointing Owner, but perhaps also even to encourage him.

Unfortunately, there are those who have what a judge recently described as an exaggerated sense of their rights, and such people can be prepared to appeal against an award simply to cause maximum inconvenience to their neighbour, without worrying too much about whether they are justified in doing so – if their blinkered vision even allows them to take an unbiased view of the situation. Such people should be told that they are bound by the Act and the award, and on no account encouraged to appeal – at least, that's my opinion.

Although an award continues to be of full effect, despite the fact that an appeal has been made, a Building Owner may be very reluctant to carry on with his work. After all, if the appeal is upheld, he might then have to undo what he had done. Nevertheless, it is sometimes in both parties' interests that work started should be carried through to completion, for example if underpinning is intended and the excavation has started. This is also true, by the way, if work has started before the proper formalities have been complied with, and it may be preferable to complete the immediate job, and then bring matters to a halt while notices are served and awards prepared.

Adjoining Owners (it is usually they who appeal, rather than Building Owners) should be persuaded – if possible – in such circumstances to agree to that element of the work proceeding to completion.

Remember that an appeal could easily take a year in the courts, and at the very least is going to hold up progress for some months. Therefore: aim to avoid any possibility of an appeal by your impeccable conduct in serving the notices and agreeing the award; avoid stressing unnecessarily to your Appointing Owner his right of appeal; work hard to discourage an over-zealous owner whose desire to appeal is not matched by the justice of his cause. If there has to be an appeal, then under Section 10 (17) your Appointing Owner has only those fourteen days already mentioned in which to enter his appeal in the County Court, if he wants to be sure of its being acceptable, although there are no doubt cases where the courts would justify themselves in accepting appeals out of time, on grounds of equity or natural justice.

You may be comforted to know that most authorities are now agreed that you do not have to stop work because an award has been appealed. What, they ask, is an injunction for? If you and/or your surveyor are perfectly confident that the award is in order, and that the appeal is merely a device to thwart you, why not call the bluff of your antagonist and keep working? If he asks the courts for an interlocutory injunction he will be at risk for costs if he eventually loses his action. It's a nice thought, but you must be sure of your ground.

There is no respondent, as such, in an appeal. I was once cited in an appeal against my Third Surveyor's award, and the judge, in dismissing me from the action, remarked that it was as if he was asked to appear before the Court of Appeal to justify his decision in a case. Nor, strictly speaking, is the other Owner a respondent: a Building Owner may well wish to appear in court to support an award which an Adjoining Owner is trying to have set aside, but I don't think that his position is truly analogous with that of a defendant. You don't have to name anyone in your approach to the courts: you simply appeal against the decision of the surveyor or surveyors. But please don't, unless absolutely necessary.

Chapter 13

Penalties

It is not always easy to enforce performance of a party wall award. There is an excellent timetable for ensuring that one is produced, with methods of dealing with dilatory or obstructive surveyors. Of course, those methods are rarely needed, because you're dealing with surveyors, who are eminently sensible, industrious and co-operative chaps. It's getting the owners and the contractors to behave that's the difficulty. My father used to say that all builders were rogues: the only difference between them was that some were likeable rogues. He didn't have a generalisation for Building Owners, but if he had done so, it would probably have referred to their speed of paying their surveyors' fees.

If you meet a real bad hat, who refuses to serve notices, to appoint a surveyor, or anything like that, there is only one solution: to apply for an injunction. There is no doubt that you'll get it, because in *Bennett* v *Howells*[1] there was only a dot missing off one 'i', more or less, yet Mrs Bennett got her injunction. To some extent these are the simpler cases. They're clear cut, and an injunction is a familiar remedy which the law will readily enforce.

The problem lies more in getting the Building Owner and/or his contractor to put right minor items of damage, or the former to pay fees due to the Adjoining Owner's Surveyor. I have already said that the surveyor should not refuse to sign an award just because he hadn't yet received his fees[2]. If you, as Building Owner's Surveyor, meet this proper response from your opposite number, it behoves you to do your best to see that your Appointing Owner pays up. Apart from moral pressure, there is one section of the Act which can assist you. It used to dwell among the untrodden ways of Part XII of the LBA, a section which there were none to praise and very few to love[3]

---

[1]   See Chapter 16.
[2]   See Chapter 6.
[3]   Wordsworth, I think.

(or at any rate use). Indeed it wasn't even the whole section, 148, but a tiny sub-section, (xix). In the new, shorter, Act it is only section 17, and therefore much more likely to be read. Taken together with section 11(8), which allows the Adjoining Owner to ask for money instead of having work carried out, it makes any sum due under the Act (except fines) summarily recoverable as a civil debt.

The LBA used to make failure to pay up or observe an award an offence punishable in the magistrates' court. That sanction is now reserved for refusing to allow entry to an authorized person or obstructing someone from doing works which he is entitled to do, under section 16.

This chapter is perhaps the best place to discuss what to do when you discover that work is well under way, or even complete, without the benefit of any procedures under the Act. As I have remarked above, if you are up against a villain, you'll need an injunction to bring him to heel, but if your neighbour is merely ignorant, lazy or absent-minded, milder measures may suffice to clear up the situation.

There is absolutely no legal basis for retrospective notices or awards, and yet they are the best method, in my opinion, for getting procedures belatedly under way. Since the alternative option for the Building Owner is to be injuncted, he should have no objection, and since the Adjoining Owner will obtain an award, with a surveyor (paid for) to look after his interests, far cheaper than by going to law, he should be equally happy.

I repeat: it's not expressly legally sanctioned, but it has my approval, and on one or two occasions the courts appear to have tacitly approved this method of dealing with party wall matters which have proceeded ahead of their proper formalities.

Chapter 14

Easements

Party wall awards have nothing to do with easements. I could end this chapter there, but that would prevent me from plugging other books, especially mine on *Trouble with the Neighbours*[1], or *Rights of Light and how to deal with them*[2], and even more especially, if you really want to learn about the subject in depth, *Gale on Easements*[3]. However, it does need a few more words to drive home the obvious, but this will be a good chapter to read if you're feeling tired, because even I can't spin the subject out for more than a couple of pages.

Since section 9 seems to make it quite clear that no award can override an easement, it might seem that my first sentence would suffice, but the fact that the RICS have felt it necessary to include a clause in their sample draft award which specifically states that 'nothing therein shall be taken to confer or affect any right to light or air or any other easement', does show that the point needs ramming home. A Building Owner should not be left with the impression that because he has an award he can ignore his neighbour's other rights, but in fact, as the side note in the RICS booklet *Party Wall Legislation and Procedure* makes clear, the clause is included more to spell out to an Adjoining Owner, unfamiliar with section 9, that his rights are unaffected.

It is, unfortunately, not only the Adjoining Owner but also his surveyor, who is all too often ignorant of section 9, or if he knows about it, he refuses to act as if he did. Surveyors frequently decline to get on with awards because 'My client' (it's the sort of surveyor who calls his Appointing Owner his client who most often makes this kind of difficulty) 'is very worried about his light and has told me not to sign an award until that's sorted out'! Point him towards

[1] Calus/Spon, Property Development Library, 1983.
[2] RICS Books,1988.
[3] Sweet and Maxwell, 15th Edition, 1986.

section 9; explain that party walls are statutory and rights of light are common law; explain that the award gives the Building Owner no right to ignore the Adjoining Owner's rights; and tell him that if he doesn't act within ten days, either you'll proceed *ex parte*, or else you will go to the Third Surveyor and ask for an award of fees against his Appointing Owner because the latter's surveyor has made the approach to the Third Surveyor necessary. That should do the trick.

Many people found the words of section 54 of the LBA hard to understand and the new wording is much closer to that of the 1930 Act. This makes it clear that if you have a window in a party wall, to which you have acquired an easement, you have every right to take down the wall and rebuild it, retaining the window and its rights.

The other area in which I suppose one ought to consider easements, before rejecting them, is in the matter of overhanging eaves and projecting footings. But for the Act, you could obtain easements to retain such features; however, under section 2(2), paragraphs (g) and (h) specifically give the Building Owner the right to cut them off if they get in the way of his building.

Easement law and party wall legislation are different: keep the two things separate.

Chapter 15

Some Party Wall Problems

When are two lots of foundations each lower than the other? Who owns a wall you paid to have built? What notice do you serve if you're constructing a lift pit adjacent to a party wall? Do you always have to serve notice if your new foundations are lower than those of the next door building? What is 'laying open'? Should the named surveyor do it all by himself? Who is exempt from the Act? What qualifies for security for expenses? Can you raise a party wall on a cantilever? Answers to me on a postcard, please.

The reason that I have lumped all these questions together in this chapter, although they may be touched on – even at some length – elsewhere in the book, is because people are not in complete agreement on the answers, and so I am putting forward not the consensus (if there is one) but my firmly held views on the correct answers, so that hereafter people can say: 'John Anstey, in the standard textbook on the subject, says . . .'. That way, we will get agreement and, as I may have remarked elsewhere, as Solon said: 'It is better that the law should be certain than that it should be just'.

Question 1: when are two lots of foundations each lower than the other? *Short answer:* when one is piled and the other is on strip foundations. *Longer answer:* if you are building a new building on piles, next door to an old building, and within the three metre (or six metre) provisions of section 6, you would naturally serve notice. Later, the older building is redeveloped on traditional foundations, which go below the pile caps (but not, of course, the piles) of the new building. Many surveyors would again serve notice, to be on the safe side, because in between the pile caps the new strip foundation would, of course, be lower than the bottom of the new adjoining structure.

I should emphasise that there is only one legal answer. The bottom of foundations is the bottom of foundations and the relative depths of pile caps and edge beams have nothing to do with it. Therefore, the new traditional founds are not, in law, below the

First redevelopment

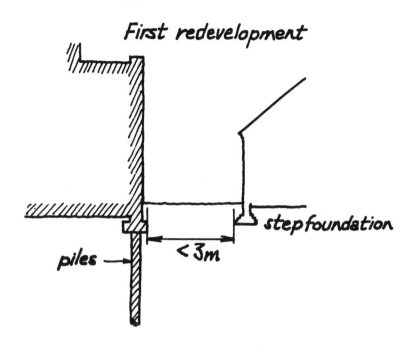

piles

step foundation

< 3m

Second redevelopment

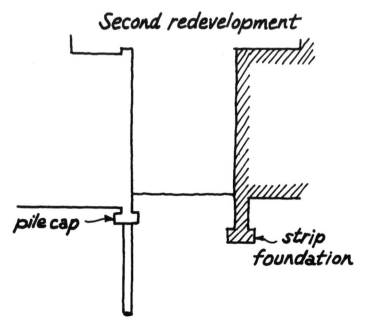

pile cap

strip foundation

Adjoining Owner's foundations. What I am saying is that in this paradoxical situation, many surveyors will behave in this way in order to have a professional acting for the Adjoining Owner, agreeing schedules and sorting out problems. He would be well advised, however, not to serve unnecessary notices which are not strictly within the Act without advising the Building Owner of the circumstances.

Question 2: who owns a wall you paid to have built? *Short answer:* according to *Gyle-Thompson*[1], the person whose land it stands on. *Longer answer:* the reason advanced by Brightman, J. for saying that Walstreet had no right to reduce the height of a party wall was that the wall stood astride the boundary, and therefore each side owned the part of the wall standing on their land. In my opinion, this was the wrong view. Even under the LBA, it was envisaged that an Adjoining Owner was going to have to pay for additional later use. In some people's opinion, that included when requiring the Building Owner to keep up a wall which he had built and paid for. The new Act explicitly recognizes this in section 2(2)(e) and (m) and section 11(7).

Question 3: what notice do you serve if you're constructing a lift pit adjacent to a party wall? *Short answer:* it all depends. *Longer answer:* it depends on whether you intend to underpin the party wall for your own purposes or not. If you do, then you serve notice under section 3, citing 2(2)(a). If you do not, but the lift pit brings you within either sub-section (1) or (2) of section 6, then you serve notice under sub-section (5) of that section. In my opinion – though others may differ – you do not need to serve twice for one lot of underpinning. However, it cannot be wrong to do so, and if you're a belt and braces man (or whatever the feminine equivalent is), by all means carry on.

Question 4: do you always have to serve notice if your new foundations are lower than those of the next door building? *Short answer:* yes. *Longer answer:* once again, it's a question of reading the words very carefully. After dealing with the basic three and six metre provisions, the section[2] concludes 'he (the Building Owner) may, and if required by the adjoining owner shall, . . . underpin or otherwise strengthen or safeguard the foundations of the building of the adjoining owner . . .'. It has been argued from this that you

---

[1]   See Chapter 16.
[2]   Section 6(1).

only need to serve notice if you propose to underpin, but just think about it. If you don't serve because you don't intend to underpin, how does the Adjoining Owner know whether to require you to do so? Therefore, dismiss the arguments of those who say that notice is only required if underpinning is proposed: serve.

A supplementary, and very reasonable, question also arises here. What if your foundations are already lower than those of next door, and you propose to rebuild on new foundations no lower, perhaps even slightly less deep than before, but still below your neighbour's? Do you still have to serve notice? The legal answer must be yes.

Question 5: what is 'laying open'?[1] *Answer:* who knows? *More helpful answer:* it doesn't matter as much as it used to do. Under the LBA, there was doubt about whether it included simply exposing the party wall to the weather. Most people thought that it did not and that one was not therefore bound to provide protection in those circumstances – although almost everybody did. In the new Act, section 2(2)(n) specifically deals with this point: you may expose the party wall, but you must weather it appropriately.

Question 6: should the named surveyor perform every single function himself? *Some people's answer:* yes. *My answer:* no. Not only does it make the fees prohibitively expensive if the highly qualified expert is going to tramp the streets trying to identify Adjoining Owners, but it also makes him less readily available to deal with the really tricky questions that demand his expertise. As I have implied in the chapter dealing with fees[2], for leg-men's work, use leg-men. Juniors are perfectly well able to do a lot of the leg work. They can take schedules, even agree the terms of awards, but they must have the authority and supervision of the named surveyor to do so. It is extremely unproductive to send out a representative who has to report back before any decisions are made. The named surveyor, however, must take full responsibility for those decisions by his assistant.

Question 7: who is exempt from the Act? *Popular long-held answer:* all those listed in section 151 of the LBA. *My answer* (supported by other top men): only those listed in sections 18 and 19. That means the properties of the Inns of Court within Inner London (i.e. which were exempt under the LBA) and those properties occuped by the Monarch, the Duke of Lancaster or the

---

[1]   Section 7(3).
[2]   See Chapter 7.

Duke of Cornwall. Land vested in the Crown, but not occupied in that way, is not exempt, so all government buildings are included.

Question 8: what qualifies for security for expenses? *Frequent answer:* any damage you fear suffering. *My answer:* only the reasonable expectation that you might be left exposed to costs through the default of the Building Owner. For example, if he proposes to lay open your premises (really lay open, under section 7(3)), it is perfectly reasonable to require the deposit of a sum which would enable you to replace the wall and enclose yourself again. You should not demand security because a scaffolder might stick a pole through your window. Section 12 is not, therefore, a general catch-all by which you can demand security because you think the Adjoining Owner's building might suffer damage and the Building Owner might be reluctant or slow to pay.

Question 9: can you raise a party wall on a cantilever? *One answer:* Richard Ellis used to say no. *My answer:* yes. This particular problem arises when you have an old party wall, which has to remain in position while you construct a new building which is going to rise to a greater height. Very often, the best structural answer to the risk of possible damage to the existing wall and its foundations is to carry the new building on its own foundations and frame, and then to construct the new, higher portion of the party wall on a beam sitting over the old wall, cantilevered out from the columns adjacent to the party wall.

I think that, in the ordinary meaning of the words, this is 'raising the party wall'. Richard Ellis said that as the new structure was not bearing directly on to the old – there is usually a compression joint between the two – it could not be said to stand on the land of two owners; and it certainly doesn't, being one party's raising, separate buildings of two owners. Therefore, they said, it could not be called raising. They were wrong (I think).

Furthermore, such is the standing of The Pyramus and Thisbe Club that an Official Referee, Judge Esyr Lewis, was prepared to hear a mock appeal on the subject, in the council chamber of the RICS. Two members set themselves up as Building and Adjoining Owners or Surveyors, and briefed two other members as Counsel. A brilliantly and succinctly argued case by the outstanding Counsel in favour of the cantilever (a well known author) persuaded the Judge that, in common sense terms, the wall was being raised, and thus satisfied the Act. Proponents of the other view have subsequently, reluctantly, accepted such raising.

A new question, 10, arose when the national Building Regulations superseded the London Building Byelaws. Although it probably should have arisen before, the change brought the problem to the fore. Since a two-hour fire resistance is all that is needed to satisfy the law, can an Adjoining Owner insist on a greater period of resistance? Opinion has not yet crystallised on the correct solution, but my view is that there are two answers. If the Building Owner is rebuilding a party wall, he cannot substitute a wall which is in any way less suitable for the Adjoining Owner's purposes than that which it replaces. On the other hand, if he is raising the party wall, for his own purposes, I suspect that he is entitled to build it as flimsily as the law allows.

Chapter 16

Some Leading Cases

Leadbetter v *Marylebone Corporation*, 1905

I don't agree with the verdict in this case, and I think it might be overturned on slightly different facts.

There are a number of interesting sidelines to *Leadbetter* which bear mention in passing, remembering that it dealt with the 1894 London Building Act, many of whose provisions have been substantially re-enacted down to 1996. Indeed, the words of the new Act are not dissimilar. The parties had had an earlier award by which the Corporation was entitled to raise the party wall in the future. When it proceeded to do so, Leadbetter got an injunction because it hadn't served notice. The judge, however, granted the injunction in terms which allowed Marylebone to proceed as soon as it had an award for its new works.

Notice was duly served but, as the parties were at such odds, it took a very long time to agree upon a Third Surveyor and get the awards made. Six months after the service of notice, there was still no award, so the plaintiffs held that the notice was now invalid, and sought execution of the earlier judgment in their favour. The defendants argued that the six months validity only applied in cases where the work was consented to, not where there was a difference. The court held that this contention was correct. If proceedings between appointed surveyors delayed matters for more than six months, it was very hard on the Building Owner if he had to start *de novo*. The words of the relevant section of the 1894 Act were: 'a party wall or structure notice shall not be available for the exercise of any right unless the work to which the notice relates is begun within six months after the service thereof' and the words of section 47(3) were very little different in 1939: 'a party structure notice shall not be effective unless the work to which the notice relates is begun within six months after the notice has been served'. I do not see any substantive difference between the two. The words of the new Act are slightly different, at section 3(2)(b), but not, I think, in substance, except for doubling the six months to twelve. 'A party structure notice shall . . . cease to have effect if the work to which it relates –

(i) has not begun within the period of twelve months beginning with the day on which notice is served . . .'.

Lord Justice Mathew held that this section only applied where no difference arose, and said that he could find no indication in the Act that the limit of six months was to apply when there was a difference. This strikes me as specious reasoning to justify an equitable decision. Marylebone thought they had the right to build, and started to do so; stopped by Leadbetter until they had obtained an award, they promptly served notice; proceedings thereafter were protracted, doubtless by Leadbetter's side, who then withdrew from negotiations and tried to secure an injunction calling for the pulling down of building to which Marylebone had tried to give legal standing. It was, therefore, I repeat, equitable to find a loophole for Marylebone. But was it right?

Examine the judgment. 'That sub-section appears to me to provide for cases in which . . . the adjoining owner consenting thereto, no difference arises . . .'. Why? Where does the section say anything about consent? The judge went on. 'I cannot see any indication in the Act that the limit of six months . . . is to apply . . . to a case where there is a difference'. Of course there isn't, because if it applies generally, there is no need to specify that it applies where there is dissent. The judge's reasoning doesn't hold water, and in my opinion the very slight change of wording after forty-five years might well have justified a modern court in holding with me, that the six months was always definitive under the 1939 Act. Under the new Act, I'm even more sure.

My advice is, if you haven't completed an award twelve months after serving notice, serve new notices.

Selby v *Whitbread*, 1917

If ever there was a case that proved how impossible it is for a Building Owner to shrug off his responsibilities, this is it. In this important leading case, the surveyors, having reserved to themselves the right to do so in their original award, made an addendum award after the land in question had been dedicated as a highway, so that the Building Owner no longer owned or controlled it: yet the addendum was held to be valid.

There was a pair of buildings in Royal Mint Street about 200 years old, and one of the pair set out to reconstruct itself thirteen feet back from its former building line. The result of this was to expose the whole height of the party wall for this distance. The original award concerned with the demolition and reconstruction had said that the Building Owner was to 'take every precaution for the support of the building of the Adjoining Owner . . .'.

Shortly after the works were completed, the now open land adjoining the party wall was sold to the LCC and the land dedicated to the public. Shortly after that, the Adjoining Owner's Surveyor wrote to ask the Building Owner's Surveyor what he proposed to do to support the party wall and the premises behind it. The Building Owners and, I am sorry to say, their Surveyor, declined to take any further action, claiming that they had offloaded their responsibility on to the LCC. The Third Surveyor was called in by Selby's Surveyor, and they made an award calling on Whitbreads to put up a substantial pier, and do some other minor works. That award was appealed.

The remarks of McCardie, J. are of great interest. He said that if a Building Owner could discharge his liabilities by selling his property to another, it would seriously diminish the rights of Adjoining Owners, and that transfer to a man of straw would deprive an Adjoining Owner of his proper remedy against the initiator of building operations. He stated that he had read with care the London Building Act, and that he found no section to allow a transfer of liability nor one that implied it. 'I should require a clear provision of the statute before holding that such a transmission of liability could take place against the will, and perchance without the knowledge, of the Adjoining Owner.' 'It seems to me,' he added, 'that that section (the one requiring security, now 12) contemplates that the person who serves the notice . . . shall be and remain liable for all the results which follow from such notice.' The jurisdiction of the surveyors remains in full force until 'the final adjustment of all questions in difference'.

I make no apology for quoting at length from this judgment, and there's more to come. It is studded with words of guidance for party wall surveyors, and it would do you no harm to read it all. It is noteworthy that the judge frequently referred to the surveyors as arbitrators, which must give some support to the arguments advanced elsewhere that that is what they are: certainly not agents for their Appointing Owners. In doing so, he emphasised that 'the primary function of the arbitrators is to safeguard the interests of the Adjoining Owner; although they must, of course, consider the rights and interests of the Building Owner'. In other words, and far too many so-called party wall surveyors forget this, both surveyors have a duty to both Owners, not only to the one that appointed them.

The next gem that I think warrants selection is the judge's comments on the validity of an award if part of it was invalid. At one time it had been considered that any defect voided the whole award. Later practice held that if the bad could be separated from the good it should be done, and the rest of the award upheld, and McCardie, J. thought that the Court should support an award rather than destroy it, if possible.

The defendants had claimed that some of the works awarded to be done were unnecessary. Even if that was so, the judge thought that the surveyors' decision on that point should be upheld, since it was a matter of expert knowledge, falling most appropriately within the jurisdiction of the arbitrators.

My final extract is also very important but, in my opinion, still open to argument. The judge held that where common law rights and party wall legislation are inconsistent, then the statutory conditions override the common law. My own view is that that is only so where a common law right is expressly excluded or overridden, such as in giving access to a neighbour's land under section 8[1], but not in taking away an Adjoining Owner's right of support, for example, just because the surveyors have the power to award how support shall be maintained. Even McCardie, J. added that a plaintiff could still bring an action if the defendant had exercised his Building Act rights negligently or improperly.

What a case. All party wall surveyors should go on pilgrimage to The Rising Sun in Royal Mint Street. And quickly: it may be about to be pulled down.

Bond v Nottingham Corporation, 1940

One reason for including this case is that I got the date wrong in my book *Trouble with the Neighbours* where I gave it, by simple

[1] See Chapter 9.

transposition, as 1904. Another is that it bears on other party wall cases, particularly *Bradburn* v *Lindsay*[1].

In this case it was held by Sir Wilfred Greene, later Lord Greene, Master of the Rolls, that an owner was 'under no obligation to repair that part of his building which provided support for his neighbour'. He could therefore eventually allow his neighbour's property to fall down although he could not, of course, do something positive to withdraw support. However, his neighbour did not have to sit by and watch his support crumble away. He could enter the next-door property and restore support himself.

This is the only case I know which gives a right of entry to a neighbour's premises, apart from party wall legislation. In London, of course, you didn't need to take advantage of Bond since, if any decay or damage threatened the party wall itself you could serve notice under what used to be section 46(1)(a), requiring both parties to contribute to the works of repair and, if necessary, you could enforce entry under what was section 53. The same now applies nationally, under section 2(2)(b) and section 8.

Phipps v *Pears*, 1964

Although one of the judges in the Court of Appeal said, *obiter*, in the case of *Marchant*[2], that he would be prepared to consider reversing *Phipps* v *Pears*, it is still good law at the time of writing. This is not strictly speaking a party wall case, but it has a great deal of relevance.

There were two old houses in Warwick. One was pulled down in about 1930, and a new house constructed abutting, but not bonded to, the remaining property. In 1962, the older property was pulled down in its turn, leaving the newer wall exposed. This wall, built against the older, was rather unsuitable for such exposure to the elements, being unrendered and unpointed. Support did not enter into it: the question was whether you could acquire an easement to protection from the wind and rain.

According to *The Times* of 11th March, 1964, the Master of the Rolls (Lord Denning), 'said that every man was entitled to pull down his own house if he liked . . . there was no such easement known to the law as an easement to be protected from the weather'. It follows from this that when a party wall is exposed, it has to be

---

[1] See below.
[2] See below.

dealt with by award whenever a wall needs it. After all, a damp party wall is no good to either owner, even if the effects are felt sooner by the Adjoining Owner.

Protection is called for in the Act when property is laid open or when a hitherto protected party wall is exposed. As to when that is, see elsewhere[1].

Gyle-Thompson v Walstreet, 1973

Walstreet served notice on Gyle-Thompson that it intended to take down the forty-foot high wall which formed the external wall of Walstreet's building at the end of Gyle-Thompson's garden, and replace it with an eight foot wall topped with a seven foot six inches slatted fence. It was admitted that the wall stood astride the boundary. The two surveyors failed to agree on the pulling down, but the Building Owner's Surveyor and the Third Surveyor made an award allowing a modified version of the proposals, which had been agreed with other parties whose gardens were similarly bounded. A fortnight after the award had been given to the Building Owner, his workmen started demolishing the wall, only to be stopped by a policeman called in by Gyle-Thompson, who soon obtained an *ex parte* injunction restraining the demolition.

It was held by Brightman, J. that even though the fourteen days had elapsed for appeal, that was not relevant if the award was fundamentally bad, which this one was. It was not therefore necessary to decide what constituted 'delivery' if, as alleged, the Adjoining Owner had not received his copy as soon as the Building Owner. On the substantive issue, he held that there was no right in the London Building Act permanently to reduce the height of a party wall and you could, therefore, only take down a party wall if you proposed to rebuild it to the same height or higher.

Several people have since effectively used this to extort very considerable payments from Building Owners anxious to lower or remove walls, even when the removal benefited the Adjoining Owners as well. I think this is immoral, and it is why the new Act allows for such lowering, in strictly controlled circumstances.

Some other matters were also dealt with in the hearing of this case. A second notice had been served, only slightly varying the works, and sent to Gyle-Thompson, care of his appointed surveyor.

---

[1]   See Chapter 15.

The judge held that this notice had not been properly served, and it would only have been so if the surveyor had been held out as an agent of the Owner. Each notice initiates a new set of proceedings, a possible new dispute and, if so, the fresh appointment of a surveyor, and therefore has to go to the owner himself.

The judge referred to the Adjoining Owners as 'owning' half of the wall, which seemed to be why he thought they could keep it up against the Building Owner's wishes, and it is on this point more than any other that I would take issue with him. The wall had almost certainly been built, if under the Act, by one Owner paying for the whole forty-foot height, or getting at the very most a garden wall sized contribution from the Adjoining Owner. A garden wall was all that the Adjoining Owners needed, wanted, or paid for. They were now asking for the benefit of a forty-foot high garden wall, for which they had not paid. Under the new Act, they would now be liable to be asked to contribute under section 11(7), for making additional use of a party wall[1], or else bound to let the wall be reduced to garden wall height. I think that the same was in fact true under the former legislation, but this point was not well argued before the court, and the costs of an appeal were too great to make the matter of principle worth pursuing.

Bennett v *Howells*, 1981

Mr Howells' architect had advised him that the wall in question was not a party wall and so, although Mrs Bennett knew what was going on, no 'formal' notice had been served. At the very last minute a certain rights of light expert who had been called in was casually asked to confirm that the wall was not party, but gave the contrary opinion. A letter was then put through Mrs Bennett's door informing her that the works would be starting in a couple of days' time and that although she had agreed that it was not a party wall, she was being given notice confirming the earlier information. Mrs Bennett did nothing until the works actually started, when she issued a writ. Eventually, surveyors were formally appointed on both sides and the Adjoining Owner's Surveyor insisted on notice being served on 'the proper forms'. Because time was of the essence, his erroneous wish was complied with, but he was already in possession of a draft award. An RIBA form, was not normally used by the

---

[1]   See Chapter 10.

Building Owner's Surveyor, who missed out a date on it. He rang the Adjoining Owner's Surveyor and asked him to insert it, was told it would be done, but the copy eventually produced in Court by Mrs Bennett was not dated!

The two surveyors agreed and signed an award, but Mrs Bennett persisted with her action. The judge held that the award was void because it was dated before the finally dated notices had been served, and that the combination of letters from architects and Building Owners could not be construed as constructive notice. He therefore awarded Mrs Bennett an injunction restraining Mr Howells from carrying out any works until proper notice was served and a new award agreed.

The extraordinary and instructive point to be learnt from this case is that the injunction actually availed Mrs Bennett nothing. Two months later, exactly the same works were carried out, in accordance with an award in exactly the same terms. Her property was not at any serious risk of damage, nor did it suffer any. All that happened was that Mr Howells was put to considerable expense, and had to put up with a building site in his kitchen for another two months. All this, because of a couple of technical flaws in procedure. One might ask whether an injunction was really appropriate in the circumstances. One should undoubtedly learn the importance of crossing every 't' and dotting every 'i', since the courts will always require the procedures to be followed precisely (as indeed Brightman, J. had specifically said in *Gyle-Thompson*).

I should tell you that Mrs Bennett disagrees with this report of the case, but has not convinced me that it contains substantial inaccuracies.

Marchant v *Capital and Counties*, 1983

In 1969, Capital and Counties redeveloped the Pantechnicon. This was an ancient storage warehouse with very substantial walls. Many, many years ago, Mrs Marchant's predecessors had built a mews cottage against the rear wall of the warehouse, using it as one wall of their building. That part of the wall against which they enclosed had become, therefore, a party wall under section 44(ii) of the LBA, now definition (b) in section 20. Capital and Counties' proposals envisaged leaving the wall standing as a boundary wall, but with no building against it on their side. Of course, they had to leave enough of it up to enclose Mrs Marchant's house.

While the works were being carried out, it was expected that there might be some exposed pockets of brickwork from which beams had been removed, and which might therefore cause some damp problems to Mrs Marchant. The two surveyors therefore agreed that these would need dealing with, and stated in their award that the Building Owner was at liberty to carry out any weatherproofing to the wall necessary while the works were being done.

Many years later, Mrs Marchant was suffering from damp in her walls and brought an action against Capital and Counties. The High Court Judge dismissed her action as being out of time, not covered by common law, and not arising out of the award. Mrs Marchant's surveyor had, unfortunately, died, but the Judge had the benefit of hearing evidence from Capital and Counties' surveyor. Mrs Marchant appealed, and the Court of Appeal, who of course did not hear evidence, decided that the surveyors meant to include the weather-proofing in the part of the award which dealt with what the Building Owner must do, and that it was meant to be a continuing liability, not just while the works were being carried out, and so Mrs Marchant's claim was not time barred!

Courts are entitled to find that documents don't mean what their authors intended them to mean, but many felt that this particular decision was taking that liberty to extremes. The important aspect of the judgments in this case is that surveyors are now held to be capable of imposing continuing liabilities on their owners by award, which was previously thought not to be the case.

Bradburn v *Lindsay,* 1983

This is a rather difficult case as to how far a neighbour's duty extends. Mrs Lindsay neglected her house, despite complaints from Mr Bradburn as early as 1972. Eventually the house was so derelict that Mrs Lindsay allowed the council to pull it down in 1977. From the earlier neglect and later exposure, the Bradburns' house got thoroughly dry-rotted, as well as exposed to weather and suffering some subsidence cracks.

The case was carefully distinguished from *Phipps* v *Pears*[1] because the two properties in the present case shared a common wall or, in the case of the roof void, a lack of it. *Bond* v *Nottingham*

---

[1]   See above.

Corporation[1], which postulated a right to self-help was also brought in, but Judge Blackett-Ord held that the right to take measures for your own benefit did not relieve another party of any duty which he might owe you (citing *Leakey* v *National Trust*, 1980). Accordingly, the Bradburns were awarded damages for the dry rot, plus reasonable works to make the 'party walls' secure against further inroads.

Brace v *SE Regional Housing Association Ltd*, 1984

The critical element of this case for party wall surveyors is only a small part of a much larger whole. The matter concerned a 'party wall' in Harrow, outside the London Building Act, but the two surveyors dealt with it more or less in accordance with 'inside the Act' procedures, by a party structure agreement.

After the Building Owner's (the Housing Association) property was pulled down, Mrs Brace noticed cracking and subsidence. One of the defendant's answers to the subsequent claim was that Mrs Brace's surveyor had agreed an 'award', and that as that award had been complied with, Mrs Brace had no further right of support.

The Court of Appeal held that entering into an agreement (and I fancy that rule might apply to an award[2]) was not to be construed as a giving up of any rights of support. If one party wished to rely upon abandonment, they would have to prove the existence of that intention in express terms, and no such terms were to be found.

It is of interest that the operative clause was in somewhat vague terms: 'The Building Owner shall be at liberty . . . to strengthen, repair or underpin' the party wall. It was therefore clearly left to the Housing Association to decide whether and how to support the wall. It might be argued that if a specific form of works had been agreed by her surveyor and accepted by the Adjoining Owner, there would have been more chance of substantiating an allegation that she had surrendered her rights. However, in an unreported (perhaps even settled out of court) case with which I was peripherally involved, inside the Act, in which nearly every procedural action was carried out incorrectly, thus complicating an already tricky situation so that, the two surveyors having perhaps never been properly appointed, their award may well have been void *ab initio*

---

[1]   See above.
[2]   Per The Lord Chancellor (in *Iolanthe*).

and its strictures thus unenforceable, it was alleged that the Adjoining Owner's Surveyor (if that's what he was in law) was liable along with the Building Owner and his Surveyor for the collapse of the Adjoining Owner's building. (I hope you followed that: I like long sentences with lots of subordinate and parenthetical clauses.) It was held or conceded, I forget which, that the prime responsibility was still that of the Building Owner.

One further sideline on this latter case. I had suggested, in the capacity of *éminence grise* or *amicus curiae*, that if the Adjoining Owner's Surveyor had been appointed under the Act, he couldn't be sued for negligence, as an arbitrator; if he hadn't been properly appointed, he had no such immunity. As far as I know, this basic contention has not been settled, but I think you would have difficulty suing a party wall surveyor.

I must close this section by reiterating the main point in *Brace*: an Adjoining Owner's rights are not lightly given away, and responsibility rests with the Building Owner unless there is strict proof to the contrary.

And that, ladies and gentlemen, is just about all I can think of to tell you about party walls, apart from the Appendices which follow, some of which are of even more marginal relevance than the asides to which you have been treated in the main body of this work. Unfortunately, whereas thirty years ago I knew everything about party walls, I now know at least three times as much, and find that I still don't know everything. Nearly every day brings some new little twist to my attention, and very salutary it is to realise that what used to be twenty-seven pages of legislation and is now only fifteen can have so many subtleties lurking within it. By the time this book reached its third edition, I hoped that I had managed to tackle nearly every problem which I or my readers had thought up. Obviously, in dealing with a new Act, even though it is going over familiar ground, I am much less sure that I have coped with everything. I reiterate the promise that has figured in every edition so far: if it runs to another, I will try to incorporate in it what I have learned in the meantime, together with any points brought up by argumentative readers.

Until then, I leave you with this admonition. Keep the Act to hand, and never be afraid or ashamed to say to a questioner: 'Just a moment while I see exactly what the Act says'. I have taken my own advice in that respect constantly while writing this book, and I only hope it has worked.

Appendix I

Un peu d'histoire
(as Michelin puts it)

When I wrote the first edition of this book, the earliest reference I could find to party walls was in the Ten Books on Architecture by Vitruvius, written around the year dot, ±50. Not everything he has to say is of immediate relevance in the world of high-tech building, but if architects were to study his advice on rights of light they would do better than they do by using their long-discredited so-called 45° rule. My wife, Rosemary, drew my attention to a passage on the subject, and to one on party walls. In this (Book III, Chapter VIII) he offers advice which conflicts, unfortunately, with section 11[1]: 'When arbitrators are appointed to value party walls, they do not value them at what they cost to build, but they look at the original contract and then deduct one eightieth of the cost for every year that the wall has been built in order to arrive at its present-day value.'

Later, the archaeologist Tim Tatton-Brown told me of the Pergamum Building By-Laws enacted in about 200 BC. After dealing with highways (width and maintenance of) and refuse (disposal of) they get down to party walls. Where repairs are needed and one party is reluctant, he has to pay three-fifths, instead of half, the cost. There is also very useful guidance on a problem we have today still not solved definitively: where both parties use a wall equally, they pay equally for its repair, but where a wall has a building on one side and an open area on the other, then the costs are defrayed in the proportion of two to one. The same rule is applied to two-storey buildings abutting single-storey ones.

It appears that notice had to be given of any works proposed to party walls, and agreement obtained, and the equivalent of a three metre notice was also needed if you wanted to dig a trench alongside the party wall. There were very complicated rules indeed about drainage channels when two properties abutted on a slope, but if you want to read about those you'll have to find a copy of *The Greeks*

---

[1]   See Chapter 10.

in Ionia and the East by J.M. Cook (Thames and Hudson, 1962). You'll also find a whole article on Roman legislation in *Structural Survey*, Vol.13 No.4 (1995), reviewing, among other books, *Ancient Rome: City Planning and Administration* by A.F. Robinson, (Routledge, 1992).

Tim, the former director of the Canterbury Archaeological Trust, also told me about a charter of 868 AD, which laid down that, in mid-ninth century Canterbury, there had to be a two-foot gap between houses to allow for eaves drip. This is the earliest written evidence for dense occupation in any town in England.

After this, my list of antiquarian references passes through a dark age until the fourteenth century: a book edited by my former history tutor, Dr Helena Chew, and William Kellaway, gives details of party wall cases heard at that time by the London Assize of Nuisance. On Friday, 22nd January, 1305, it was held that the 'custom of the City does not permit anyone, even though having a share in a stone wall, to demolish his part of it without the consent of his coparcener'. Just like *Gyle-Thompson* v *Walstreet*! However, in May 1324, it was held that the Building Owner could use a bearing in the wall to the depth of his ownership, and no more.

Many of the disputes arose out of the *Lex de Assisa*, which originated around 1200 and laid down, for example, rather like section 1, that for stone walls three feet thick, each party was to give eighteen inches of his land and half the cost. If one party could not or would not build jointly, he had to give all the three feet of land necessary, the other party built and paid for the wall, and its ownership was then shared.

In 1333, a suit was brought for the rebuilding of a party wall between two privies. The plaintiffs said that 'the extremities of those sitting upon the seats can be seen, a thing which is abominable'. It was ordered, after a site inspection(!), that the wall should be replaced.

Keith McDonald found a reference to a party wall dispute in Dartmouth, with an award dated 1st March, 1429. This held that the Building Owner should take down the pynon wall (a gable) to floor level, and rebuild it of sufficient strength for his purposes at his own expense, supporting the Adjoining Owner's premises the while. Thereafter the wall was to be maintained jointly. Sadly, party walls then left the West Country, except for a lingering presence in Bristol, which had its own Building Act till recently, though it didn't seem to be much used even by Bristolians.

It is not surprising that the Great Fire of London, with its rapid spread, should have led to an Act to control various aspects of building in the City. The Act of 1667 also dealt with a few party wall matters, including agreement between surveyors that party wall foundations had been correctly laid out, and also the provision for payment of a half share of the costs by the Adjoining Owner – plus six per cent per annum.

In 1724 an Act was passed which extended control to the cities of both London and Westminster, and to four contiguous parishes. This introduced the idea of the Building Owner giving notice, workmen from both sides arriving at a kind of award, and then work proceeding. The 1764 Act prohibited cutting into party walls for chimneys – very much an anti-fire provision – and this was followed by another Act in the following year which first allowed forcible entry into an Adjoining Owner's premises, armed with an authority from a Justice of the Peace, in order to prevent wilful obstruction (by a difficult neighbour) of reasonable works to a party wall.

The Third Surveyor, except that he is a fifth, appeared in 1772. Two surveyors or able workmen were to be appointed by each side, and a JP had the power to appoint an additional one to help the two sides/four men to come to an agreement.

The world of the party wall was substantially enlarged in 1844, when the Building Act concerned itself with 'The Metropolis', an area slightly larger than the County of London. This Act dealt at length with party walls, and virtually all its provisions, together with those of succeeding Acts, were incorporated in the 1894 Act, which we tend to look upon as the real ancestor of our present Acts since, although worded differently, the principles of that Act constitute most of what we know today.

A major recasting of the Act took place in 1930, amending legislation was passed in 1935, and in 1939 there came that paragon of Acts (well, paragonnish), The London Building Acts (Amendment) Act. Although Greater London was formed in 1965, the control of the Act was not extended beyond the former County of London where the writ of 1939 ran; but, fortunately, the abolition of Greater London in 1986 contrariwise did not reduce its sway. Many of the provisions of the 1939 Act did disappear with the GLC, including the ever-to-be-lamented District Surveyor service, but Part VI rolled on.

Finally (for the time being), the rest of England and Wales woke up to what it was missing – with a little prompting from public

113

spirited chaps like me – and the 1996 Act was passed, based very largely on the LBA. Most of the differences have been pointed out during the earlier part of this book, but the spirit of the London Building Acts lives on in the new legislation, to the great benefit of Building Owners, Adjoining Owners and party wall surveyors.

Appendix II
Who Does What

I thought that it might be helpful to have a table of who is required to, or has the right to, do what, since it varies between Owner and surveyor. Of course, the surveyor can do things on behalf of the Owner as his agent, but he must be expressly authorised to do so.

Section	Action	Doer
1(2)	Serve notice	Building Owner
(3)	Consent	Adjoining Owner
(5)	Serve notice	Building Owner
3(1)	Serve notice	Building Owner
(3)(a)	Consent	Adjoining Owner
4(1)	Counter notice	Adjoining Owner
5	Consent	Adjoining Owner
6(5)	Serve notice	Building Owner
(7)	Consent	Adjoining Owner
(9)	Supply particulars	Building Owner
8(1)	Enter premises	Building Owner, his servants, agents and workmen
(2)	Enter closed premises	As 8(1), plus a policeman
(3)	Notice of entry	Building Owner
(5)	Entry	Surveyor
10(1)(a)	Concur in appointment	Both Owners
(b)	Appoint surveyor	Each Owner
(3)	Agreed surveyor fails	Start again
(4)	Either Owner fails to appoint	The other Owner
(5)	Exit of a surveyor	Original Appointing Owner
(6)	Surveyor refuses to act	Other surveyor *ex parte*
(7)	Surveyor fails to act	Other surveyor *ex parte*
(8)	Surveyor fails or refuses to agree a Third Surveyor	Either surveyor

Section	Action	Doer
(9)	Third Surveyor fails	The other two surveyors
(10)	Award	Two surveyors or, rarely, one or three
(11)	Disputed Award	Third Surveyor, at the request of either party or either surveyor
(13)	Costs of award	Surveyors decide, parties pay
(17)	Appeal	Either Owner
11	Expenses	Either Owner, or as settled in the award
12	Security for expenses	The Owners
13	Account for expenses	The Owners

It is worth noting that very little falls to the surveyors: their only function under the Act is to draw up the award. As I have remarked, however, the surveyor very often does a great deal more, acting as the agent for his Appointing Owner and outside his arbitratory function. In such case, he must be absolutely certain that he has the requisite authority to do so, and if he can wrap it all up in his letter of appointment, so much the better.

Appendix III

Section 10 Timetable

Much of this already appears elsewhere but it may help to have it tabulated.

Action	*Time*
An Agreed Surveyor to act after written request	10 days
Either party to appoint a surveyor after written request	10 days
Either surveyor to act after written request by either party or the other surveyor	10 days
Third Surveyor to act after written request	10 days
Either party to appeal	14 days

Appendix IV
Idle Jottings

Schedules of Condition

This, by the way, is a shibboleth. Educated party wall surveyors speak of schedules (plural) of condition (singular). Less well brought up chaps speak of conditions (plural). A property may have many rooms, but only one condition.

What is the purpose of an S of C? It is to record the state of those parts of an adjoining building which might be affected by the Building Owner's works. Do not record that the wallpaper is sky-blue pink: even the worst contractor is not likely to sneak in and paint it green overnight. Do say whether it is damp stained or torn by plaster cracking below it: that is the sort of thing the Adjoining Owner never notices until work starts next door. He then swears – and believes – that the damage was caused by the works.

Note the extent of any existing cracks, and whether they appear to be superficial or to penetrate the fabric of the structure. If necessary, put tell-tales or pencil marks on them. Buy a crack gauge from The Pyramus and Thisbe Club. Count the broken window panes.

It is difficult to know how far to take your Schedule. Certainly you must cover the party wall itself and then probably extend into the room, via ceiling, floor and flank walls, up to the first natural break – a window, door, or where there is a change of surface. Such is the nature of the beast, that sometimes you won't have anticipated where the damage will break out. In King's Cross Road there were, for nearly twenty years, signs of damage to the next building but one from a development with which I was concerned, because the immediately adjacent building was so solid that when it moved – which it did quite enthusiastically – it moved as a whole. No one, of course, had thought of taking a Schedule of the building next door nor, in my opinion, should you. When that sort of thing happens, you just have to use your surveyor's common sense to sort the damage out and attribute blame appropriately.

Don't rely on photographs. Unless they are very skilfully taken – and not always then – they won't show up the faint cracks that need to be recorded. Use them as *aides-mémoires* by all means, perhaps overdrawing on them to indicate the position of a crack, but sketches are probably just as good if not better.

Presentation is a matter of taste. I prefer the method illustrated in the RICS handbook – in fact, I think that's one of my Schedules. Choose your own style by all means, but always remember that its purpose is to make it easy to recall the original condition of the premises, to be able readily to identify any changes, and to apportion liability.

Agent, Arbitrator, or Agitator

During the course of a party wall affair, the surveyor may be any or all of these characters. In serving notices, the Building Owner's Surveyor will probably be the first. In trying to get damage put right the Adjoining Owner's Surveyor may well have to be the last.

The important thing to remember is that most of the time, both surveyors must take on the middle role. The judge in *Selby* v *Whitbread* referred to the pair of them as arbitrators, and so they are: both conscious of both owners' rights and duties, and not acting – when they have their party wall hats on – as agents for the party who appointed them.

You will have noticed how frequently I use the term 'Appointing Owner' and how infrequently the word 'client' appears. It is more easy to preserve the correct detachment if you always refer to your Appointing Owner, and avoid calling him your client. As I have remarked elsewhere: if you can be said to have a client at all, it is the Act itself.

Appendix V

The Pyramus and Thisbe Club

What on earth, you may ask, does 'The Pyramus and Thisbe Club' have to do with surveying? Most of its members don't understand its title either, and refer to it as 'The P & T'. The relevance, however, is that Pyramus and Thisbe had to converse through a chink in a wall which separated the lands of their respective fathers and, in Shakespeare's version of the lamentable comedy, performed by the rude mechanicals to honour the wedding of Theseus and Hippolyta in *A Midsummer Night's Dream*, Bottom tells Theseus that, 'The wall is down that parted their fathers'. This is the motto of the club which, you may no longer be surprised to learn, is concerned with party wall matters.

The club was founded soon after the case of *Gyle-Thompson* v *Walstreet*, when many imperfect reports of the judgment in that case were circulating, and it was suggested to me by two members of my staff, Colin Banyard and Mike Bailey, that there ought to be some forum in which interesting cases could be discussed and points of difference thrashed out. I immediately acted on this suggestion and wrote to every surveyor with whom I had had party wall dealings and invited them to a get-together to discuss the formation of a club. The response was enthusiastic, and unanimous agreement was reached on nearly every point except the title. A steering committee was elected, with me as the inaugural chairman, and told to set up the club on the lines discussed, and to find a generally acceptable name. I was recounting all this to an English teacher friend, Paula Morris, who suggested Pyramus and Thisbe, which so delighted me by its aptness that I positively insisted on its adoption by a confused and largely uncomprehending membership.

A couple of years later, we decided that the members ought to know under whose colours they were parading, and so a cast containing the then Master of the Worshipful Company of Chartered Surveyors, Alan Gillett; a past president of the Building Surveyors Division of the RICS, Tony Poole; the founder chairman;

and others, presented a substantial chunk of Act V to a wondering audience. To celebrate the passing of the 1996 Act, a further production was mounted with a different cast.

The club is, on the whole, a serious working body for the improvement of knowledge and understanding of party walls and associated subjects, and has attracted numerous distinguished speakers from the fields of law and engineering, as well as surveying, including Sir Desmond Heap, Michael Hart (counsel for Gyle-Thompson), Richard Pryor QC, John Earl of the Historic Buildings Division of the GLC, Trevor Aldridge QC, and others. There have been debates on contentious points, Brains Trusts, lectures from members, and practical demonstrations. The club mounted a seminar on party walls for Calus, and contributed the bulk of the working party which produced the RICS handbook.

The only qualification for membership is an active interest in party walls – no profession is excluded, and no exam has to be passed. Some architects and some engineers belong, as do several former District Surveyors, and every grade of building surveyor from trainee to President of the Division.

The Christmas lunch of the Club is usually well attended, by the President of the RICS, the Divisional President, The Chairman of the District Surveyors Association and other luminaries including occasionally the more enlightened Presidents of the RIBA. An entertainment was provided every year until 1995 (originally at the suggestion of John Whittaker) in which parodies written by Alan Gillett and myself were sung by ourselves and two or three excellent professional singers of the opposite sex, all introduced by John Anderson.

In 1989, the Club set up a working party to report on various vexed questions of interpretation of the Act, and also to make suggestions as to possible improvements.

The group (Donald Ensom, Eric Roe, the late Patrick Ellis and myself) produced a complete report, and took counsel's opinions on some knotty legal points. The results were published in a green covered booklet and then debated by the entire membership. Their views were all recorded and a definitive book for general sale was duly produced, also with a green cover and hence known as 'The Green Book'. A second edition of that work is already in preparation.

It was, of course, another working party from the club which drafted the new Act, with Alex Schatunowski and the Chairman pro tem of the Club added to the three surviving members. Later, the former District Surveyor Bruce Cox was added, together with the sponsoring peer, the Earl of Lytton, who took over from Lord Lucas (who had instigated the whole thing) when the latter became a government minister.

I'm not sure that much of the above isn't out of place, even in this book, but I think that it is probably worth giving you a fairly full idea of the club's nature. The important thing is, however, that it really is a fount of party wall wisdom and opinion, though not always the same opinion, and anyone with an obscure problem could be sure of assistance by contacting the Club, through the RICS if necessary. There will always be someone prepared to advise a fellow professional in distress.

Very Select Bibliography

Party Wall Legislation and Procedure (Fourth Edition) (RICS Books, 1996)

The Party Wall etc. Act: A Commentary (The Pyramus and Thisbe Club, 1996)

The Collected Papers of The Pyramus and Thisbe Club, 1974–94 (The Pyramus and Thisbe Club, 1996)

Anstey J. *Boundary Disputes and How To Resolve Them* (RICS Books, 1990)

Anstey J. *Access To Neighbouring Land Act, 1992* (College of Estate Management, 1993)

Anderson J., Anstey J., Hurst L. and Lord Lytton *The Party Wall etc. Act 1996* (Owlion Audio Programme, 1996)

Index

draft award 38–9, 54–61
drawings and plans 31–4, 35, 47–8, 57–8, 61, 62, 119
duties and responsibilities of owners *see* Adjoining Owner, Building Owner

easements 45, 60, 92–3, 104–5
eaves and overhanging parts 30, 93
Ellis, Patrick 121
emergency access 52, 72
enclosing 22–5, 80, 107–8
engineer 35, 40, 57
    fees 45, 75–6
Ensom, Donald 14, 69, 121
entry *see* access
estimate for fees 64, 65–6
ex parte award 19, 61, 93
excavation 31, 48, 72
    see also foundations
exemptions from Act 97–8
expenses 28, 45, 75–82
    apportionment in 200 BC 111
    security for 80–2, 83–4, 98
    see also fees
exposure 104–5
    see also laying open
external wall 26, 27, 34
extremities, exposed (1333) 112

fees 37, 46, 60, 64–6, 75–6, 90
    AO's Surveyor's 11, 46, 60, 67, 75
    engineers' 45, 75–6
    solicitors' 75
    Third Surveyor's 69
final inspection 42, 46
fire resistance 99
flats 25, 50–1
floor/ceiling partitions 25
flues *see* chimneys and flues
footings 22, 30, 77, 93
forms and letters, RICS draft 35, 36, 43, 44–5, 47
foundations 22, 31–4, 35
    Building Owner's right to put 34
    depth of 94–6, 96–7
    Foundation Award 62
    notice 53, 96–7
    safeguarding 33, 76, 96
    see also special foundations

garden wall 24, 25, 29, 30, 76, 105–6
GLC (Greater London Council) 7, 14, 55, 113
government buildings 98
'Green Book', The 121
Gyle-Thompson v *Walstreet* (1973) 26, 29, 87, 96, 105–6, 120
    a historical precedent 112

horizontal structures 25
hours of working 59

impartiality 15, 16, 19, 43, 119
incapability, surveyor's 16–17
inconvenience 78–9
increased use 80, 96, 106
injunction 89, 90, 91
    examples of use 105, 106–7
Inns of Court 97
interest on security money 82

juniors *see* assistants

laying open 97, 98
    see also exposure
LBA (London Building Acts (Amendment) Act, 1939) 7, 113–14
    on additional use 96
    on definition of party structure 25
    on easements 93
    on exemptions 97
    on laying open 97
    on penalties 90–1
    on right of entry for repair 104
    on serving notice 49
    on time limit for Third Surveyor's award 68
    on time limit to notice 100
Leadbetter v *Marylebone Corporation* (1905) 81, 100–1
Leakey v *National Trust* (1980) 109
leaseholder 20, 49, 50–1, 80
leg-men *see* assistants
letter of appointment, surveyor's 43, 44–5, 68, 116
letter of authority 35, 45, 48
letters and forms, RICS draft 35, 36, 43, 44–5, 47
Lewis, Judge Esyr 98

129